The Work of Music and
the Problem of Its Identity

Roman Ingarden

The Work of Music and the Problem of Its Identity

Translated from the original
Polish by Adam Czerniawski
Edited by Jean G. Harrell

University of California Press

Berkeley   Los Angeles

£C

University of California Press
Berkeley and Los Angeles, California

© 1986 by
Jean Gabbert Harrell

Library of Congress Cataloging-in-Publication Data
Ingarden, Roman, 1893–
    The work of music and the problem of its identity.
    Translation of: Utwór muzyczny i sprawa jego tożsamości.
    "Works by Roman Ingarden in English translation": p.
    Includes index.
    1. Music—Philosophy and aesthetics. 2. Musical form.
I. Czerniawski, Adam, 1934–   . II. Harrell, Jean G.
(Jean Gabbert), 1921–   . III. Title.
ML3845.I5713   1986   780'.1   85-24597
ISBN 0-520-05529-2 (alk. paper)

Translated from Utwór muzyczny i sprawa jego tożsamości
© Copyright by Państwowe Wydawnictwo
Naukowe, Warszawa 1966

Printed in the United States of America

1 2 3 4 5 6 7 8 9

Contents

Translator's Preface

In English-speaking countries the Polish philosopher Roman Ingarden (1893–1970) was for many years known dimly, if at all, as the author of *Das literarische Kunstwerk*. Awareness of his achievement increased significantly when an English version of this, his most important work in aesthetics, appeared, together with a translation of the companion volume, *The Cognition of the Literary Work of Art*. Also, as the bibliography below testifies without claiming completeness, commentaries on his work are increasing in number and scope.

All this material is concerned exclusively with literature. As befits a philosopher who can claim a greater involvement with aesthetics than any other twentieth-century thinker of comparable stature, however, Ingarden also investigated other arts, notably painting, architecture, music, and film. Significantly, in the interests of a unified aesthetic theory the present essay on music was originally intended to form, along with the separately published essays on architecture and painting, part of *The Literary Work of Art*.

Perhaps Ingarden's most important contribution to aesthetic theory—it certainly dominates all commentaries on his work—is his conclusion that a literary work is a stratified structure. So the work of music presents him with a special challenge when he has to conclude that it is a single-layered art and therefore in this respect categorially different from a literary work. One of the most daunting features of theorizing in aesthetics is the need to embrace a gamut of works in such diverse media, and for that reason all rigid definitions of a work of art have so far failed. Ingarden is wise enough not to be perturbed unduly by this counter-example to his stratification thesis. Ingarden's wisdom extends to his whole approach to the aesthetics of musical works. Thus, he keeps clear of biography, creativity, listeners' psychological reactions, music's expressiveness and "meaning," and the social role of music in shaping the minds of worshipers, soldiers, workers, or teenagers. He realizes, as regrettably few ever do, that art works, though "heteronomous," are objectively "out there," interesting in themselves and deserving of our respect. He therefore concentrates on elucidating what works of art *are* and rightly ignores the question of how they come about and what they do or are supposed to do to us or for us. Consequently, his chief interest lies in the musical work's structure, identity, and ontic status.

Aristotle's seemingly banal postulate that a work of art should have "a beginning, a middle and an end" is in fact profound and difficult to apply to specific works. It appears that a musical work is both easier to judge by these criteria—in that musical rules of composition demonstrate an a priori determination—and more difficult—in that musical works are very often divided into discrete "movements." It is on this latter difficulty that Ingarden concentrates, citing as an "impossible" case the following "composition": the first movement of Beethoven's Fifth Symphony, followed by a Debussy symphonic poem, followed by a Bach toccata, and ending with an orchestral transcription of an aria from Act III of Puccini's *Madame Butterfly*.

As always with such examples, a negative one looks more persuasive than positive ones. And I for one have grave doubts about the cohesion of many classical sonata-form works, including many chamber and symphonic works by Mozart, Beethoven, and Schubert, in which the third and fourth movements especially strike me as arbitrarily conjoined and interchangeable. The few examples of success include Mozart's Clarinet Quintet, his G Minor and *Jupiter* symphonies, Beethoven's Third Symphony, his last piano sonatas, Schubert's *Unfinished Symphony* (*sic!*), and (*pace* Teutonic musicologists) Chopin's piano sonatas opuses 35 and 58. Musicologists, both Teutonic and non-Teutonic, will at once point to the cohesion established by key relationships, one dramatic and compelling test being surely that, whereas pupils and scholars do not usually attempt to finish a master's painting, completion of a musical work (Schubert's Eighth Symphony, Mahler's Tenth Symphony, Bartok's Viola Concerto) is possible and aesthetically acceptable, precisely because the overall structure is much easier to discern. There is an almost logical inference from the available harmonies, rhythms, and instrumental mixes to the putative completions, and this is not after all surprising, in view of the predominantly mathematical nature of musical composition.

Unfortunately for musicologists and their apologists, rules of harmony and composition are not sufficient to guarantee aesthetic coherence. Otherwise we would have a surfeit of masterly compositions by professors of harmony. Hence the problem first noted by Aristotle, hence the rejection by listeners of scholarly completions of Schubert's *Unfinished*.

Ingarden appears tacitly to side with the musicologists. One important reason may be that he relies on a traditional set of examples, where harmonic structuring is much more orderly than it is in late twentieth-century music with its acceptance of chance elements and preference for tonal coloring over harmonic order.

It may, moreover, be argued that Schubert's *Unfinished* is a tendentious example. For here we have surviving two consecutive, fully scored movements. Imagine, on the other hand, that all we have of Beethoven's Third Symphony are (1) the first movement without the development section, (2) no trace of the second movement, (3) a piano score of the third movement, and (4) a few sketches of the fourth movement. We could, I suppose, just about accept someone reconstructing the development of the first movement and the scoring of the third movement, and possibly accept conjectures for the finale. But, granted the knowledge we actually have, would anyone have produced a score even remotely resembling the second movement funeral march? So a suitably wary musicologist would offer us a three-movement work with a conjectured gap of some fifteen minutes. Ingarden painstakingly analyzes the permissible time-lags between movements, and concludes that a break of more than a minute or two is not one likely to sustain us in the belief that we have listened through a single work. John Cage's *4'33"* of silence has, of course, a quite different end in view.[1]

On the whole, despite persuasive-looking arguments to the contrary, we should leave masters' sketches unfinished and unperformed. The point is illuminated if once again we resort to a comparison with pictorial art. No one ever dreams of rounding off drawings and sketches and filling them in with the master's favorite pigments. Why not? Principally because the sketches themselves are in a sense complete.[2] In other words, the notion of completeness operates

1. Cage's *4'33"*, and indeed his other experiments involving natural sounds, are pertinent in another sense: namely, in that they challenge Ingarden's brisk dismissal of these sounds as irrelevant to musical experience. Nor, understandably, given the time Ingarden wrote this essay, does he address himself to ontic problems posed by electronic and aleatoric music.

2. There is also the serious practical difficulty that, whereas the completion of a score does not in any way "damage" the original fragment, an

differently here. A preparatory drawing for a painting can have an autonomy a musical sketch can never achieve. Even works like Sir Joshua Reynolds's *Sketch of a Girl* (Dulwich Gallery, London) and Gustave Moreau's *Helen at the Gates of Troy* (Musée Gustave Moreau, Paris), not drawings but paintings with the pigmentation half-finished—and therefore in theory looking more "unfinished" than drawings— are thought qualified for exhibition. And their effect is particularly striking in that they appear to represent a new development in these artists' work. The thickly laden blurred pigmentations, standing in such contrast to the precise "finished" styles we associate with the main body of work by Reynolds and Moreau, portend an "impressionism," or a "fauvism" even, that we do not normally attribute to either of them.

This contrast is explicable in terms of the fact, noted by Ingarden, that the score as such is not part of the musical work. It is a set of instructions as to how the music should sound, and if there are lacunae in the instructions, these can only indicate periods of silence. This state of affairs points to a second fact that music, like literature, is a temporal art, whereas pictorial arts are spatial. The mind can complete details missing from an outline of, say, a human figure, but it cannot fill in a temporal gap of an appreciable length. This is partly due to the psychological limits of the imagination but also to the fact—carefully analyzed by Ingarden—that in a

---

attempt to saturate a drawing with paint is irreversible. In other words, we are reminded that, in Nelson Goodman's terminology, painting is an "autographic" art, whereas music is "allographic." A special skill with pencil or brush stamps an image as unmistakably by Botticelli, Poussin, or Vermeer, but no comparable masterly individuality is required from someone filling in bar lines with musical notation. Perhaps, ultimately, it is their inability to note fully this distinction that tempts musicologists to pretend they are masters.

temporal art silences are after all an integral element in the production of sounds, and silence begins to lose its significance much earlier than does a line that peters out in a drawing.

But the most important consequence of music being an allographic art concerns the musical work's ontology and identity and leads to three interrelated, intriguing puzzles that Ingarden patiently unravels: (1) There is the enduring, fixed musical score, which, however, does not constitute the musical experience and, indeed, is not even a part of that experience; (2) there is the potentially infinite set of performances, each a distinct and unique musical experience, but all, however different from one another, deriving their authority from the score; yet (3) none is judged to be the absolute, faultless, genuine embodiment of the score.

It is in fact Ingarden's thesis that such a perfect embodiment is chimerical, not so much because we live in an imperfect world, but because it is in the nature of the score that it should leave room for various interpretations, many of them unforeseen even by the composer. So where is the musical work? It comes into existence heteronomously via the intentional acts of performers and listeners. In between performances it lies dormant in the score, a Brünnhilde awaiting a Siegfried, or rather a Brünnhilde responding variously to a succession of heroes—curious mode of existence not to be countenanced by wielders of Ockham's razor. But Ingarden is not one to be frightened off by philosophical muggers. And rightly so, for musical works, as Ingarden subtly and exhaustively demonstrates, cannot be categorized in ways that would satisfy simpleminded physicalists or even simpleminded mentalists.

But is it not rather the case that the score is an accident of history, that modern high-fidelity recordings, together with

the vast capabilities of absolutely precise electronic pro-
ducers of synthetic sound, force us to rethink the whole
problem? Ingarden insists on a contrast between musical
works and paintings, the latter being concrete individuals,
the former, sets of qualities. But is not a recording a concrete
individual with invariant sounding and nonsounding properties, analogous to a painting with its invariant pigments,
shapes, and proportions? Yet even if we were to accept
the particular recording (or other mechanical method from
which variability or performance was totally excluded) as
embodying the work exhaustively, the analogy would still
not be complete, for we can have an infinite number of press-
ings of the same record, while we cannot reproduce a painting exhaustively even once. But, more fundamentally, as we
have already seen, Ingarden rejects the notion of the unique
perfect performance, and where scores exist as the reference
point, he is surely right.

But what of works for which we have no scores? This
sounds like an easy question. For if we consider works of the
past, they are not irretrievable (unless preserved—how accurately?—only in folk memory) and if we consider more
recent recorded works of which the scores have perished, we
can recreate the score with reasonable accuracy, depending
on how highly we judge the authenticity of the particular
recording or recordings, though there is of course danger of
a circular procedure in such retrieval. But the crucial point is
that once we have reconstructed the score, we are back to the
relationship of score to performances that forms the crux of
Ingarden's analysis.

Nevertheless, an important problem remains. The examples Ingarden discusses are works in the Western classical
tradition by Bach, Beethoven, Chopin, Szymanowski, and
Stravinsky. Popular music merits only a passing reference to

ephemeral folk songs. It is here, however, rather than in the classical repertoire, that modern recording techniques affect the debate dramatically.

We now have preserved on record various "folk" ephemera—early jazz, Louis Armstrong, Billie Holiday, "Fats" Waller, Marlene Dietrich, and the Beatles, to mention but a few of vast and constantly growing numbers of recorded performers.[3] In all these cases we treasure the specific performances, and even the boxed sound of the early preelectric acoustic recordings contributes to the overall effect. Here we do not care about the scores (in the rare cases where they exist) and do not take the trouble to create them where they are lost or—since much of this music is improvised—have never existed. So we do not compare performance with score, there is no score as a final arbiter, there is no tension set up between an enduring set of instructions and a succession of interpretations. It is the specific performance by Armstrong or Dietrich that constitutes the work, in a way that a specific performance by a Rubinstein or a Menuhin or a Jessye Norman or the Vienna Philharmonic does not constitute the Chopin prelude, the Bach partita, the Duparc song, or the Beethoven symphony.

So it appears that Ingarden's elitism has a serious consequence for his analysis of the musical work. By ignoring

---

3. "Pop" has of course little relation to "folk," and I use the term only as a point of reference to Ingarden's text. "Folk," in the proper sense as used by Ingarden, in fact introduces another variant into the debate about the ontic status of musical works. There are no scores, yet folk memory provides a mental equivalent to the score and in that sense "folk" is closer to high culture than to "pop," in that the work takes precedence over both composer and performer. On the other hand, since all the performer has is an aural tradition, his performances are like gramophone recordings in that they attempt faithfully to reenact the performances of previous generations.

popular works, he fails to realize that the o tic status of a musical work is a variable, since at the popul r end, and as a result of modern technology, its identity is uncomplicated by any score/performance relationship. This point is worth pressing further, because it has curious and unexpected consequences for the populist–elitist debate. Marxists and Roland Barthes, joined in a bizarre alliance of puritanism and hedonism, have recently been proclaiming vigorously the death of authors in order to cut them down to size and demystify their pretensions to arcane knowledge. They are, it seems, like the rest of us: toilers and laborers, the direction of their efforts determined by prevailing linguistic and social forces and inner compulsions. Ignorant of history, these theorists do not seem to be aware that at the dawn of aesthetic speculation Socrates had already killed the poet in the *Ion,* though of course his motivation was different. What has misled them are the claims to genius popularized at one specific point in history by early nineteenth-century poets and philosophers.

The primacy of the score, which Ingarden argues for, implies the composer's "death." He repeatedly stresses that the composer's own interpretation is not absolutely authoritative. The composer may have been in bad form when he played that particular piece (assuming it was a piece for a single instrument which he could play competently), or he may have played it excellently on many occasions but interpreted the score differently each time. Ingarden also and rightly envisages interpretations (faithful to the score) undreamed of by the composer. The score is after all a public notation: anyone can use it, anyone can "read" it. And this analogy with literature is not fortuitous. A poet uses public language and ought not to be surprised if readers interpret his metaphors in ways he had not anticipated, if their competence in synonymy is greater than his, if subsequent shifts in cultural or religious awareness import new glosses onto his seemingly unambiguous phrases. Although Ingarden does not perhaps put the case clearly enough, it must be stressed that while his argument for the score as vehicle for infinite interpretations appears to be based on an accumulation of empirical evidence, it is in fact a conceptual one, and this conclusion leads him to the designation of musical works as "intentional" and "heteronomous" in contrast to "real," "autonomous," physical, and mental objects like chairs and emotions.

In popular music, on the other hand, what counts, as we have observed, is preserved in the performance as such. The stars, the vocalists, the showpeople create the video-recordings—perhaps in one day in three dimensions with authentic smells oozing from the speakers as well. Their audiences do not fret over points of interpretation, for there is no higher authority to invoke. What matters is the showmanship, for which the music is, as it were, but an excuse. The cult of genius, the cult of personality, reigns supreme. Such is popular music, and its nature ought to make Marxists and certain post-structuralists despair.

It is of course true that devotees of high culture also can succumb to personality cults, but the score is always there to force them to acknowledge the supremacy of the work over both composer and performer. Those who cultivate Rubinstein's Chopin sooner or later admit the alternative virtues of a Vásáry or a Perahia and, if they reflect on this fact sufficiently, accept the soundness of Ingarden's arguments.

Adam Czerniawski
Dulwich, July 1984

Introduction

The starting point for our reflections upon the musical work will be the unsystematized convictions that we encounter in daily life in our communion with musical works before we succumb to one particular theory or another. Naturally, I do not intend in advance to accept these convictions as true. On the contrary, I shall submit them to critical investigations at specific points. But, for the moment at least, they must indicate the direction of further investigations. For how else could this direction be indicated? These convictions, although naively acquired and perhaps burdened with various mistakes, do after all stem from an immediate aesthetic communion with musical works, a communion that furnishes us, or at least may furnish us, with an ultimate experience of those works, thus endowing with truth the views that match the given of the experience. However fully developed, every theory of musical works that is not mere speculation but seeks a base in concrete facts must refer to the presystematic convictions that initially gave direction to the search. It seems that there is another reason why we must refer to the given of the immediate musical experience. It is that various theories in the realm of so-called aesthetics or the psychology of music are conditioned too powerfully by the general state of philosophy and of sciences particular to a given epoch and therefore too heavily burdened with theoretical prejudices that make it difficult to reach the experientially given facts. In addition I intend to discuss various problems which have not been raised within the existing literature on musical theory.

The convictions I wish to refer to are the following:

The composer fashions his work in a creative effort, over a certain period of time. This labor fashions something—the musical work in fact—that previously did not exist but from the moment of its coming into being does somehow exist quite independently of whether anyone performs it, listens to it, or takes any interest in it whatever. The musical work does not form any part of mental existence, and, in particular, no part of the conscious experiences of its creator: after all, it continues to exist even when the composer is dead. Nor does it form any part of the listeners' conscious experiences while listening, for the work of music continues to exist after these experiences have ceased.

Moreover, so it is said, the musical work is not identified with its various performances. Despite this difference, the performances resemble the particular work, and the more they resemble it the "better" they are. The performance of a musical work reveals it to us in its characteristics and in the whole sequence of its parts. Finally, the work is totally different from its score. It is mainly or wholly a sounding work, while the notation of the score is simply a defined arrangement, usually of graphic signs.

These views may appear to us trivial and obvious; nevertheless, we have to examine them critically, especially since they lead to considerable difficulties.

Let us take as example a certain work we all know, say, Chopin's B Minor Sonata. What is the situation? According to earlier assertions the sonata is different both from the experiences of its composer (Chopin) and from the experiences of innumerable listeners who have heard it. At the same time it appears that the sonata is not material (physical). And yet how can a thing exist if it is not mental (pertaining to consciousness) or physical and can exist even when no

one takes any conscious interest in it? Or take another problem: it is said that each time we hear that sonata in a particular performance we hear the *same* sonata even though it is in
every case a new and somewhat different performance, since
the performer and the conditions are different. How can it
possibly be that in different performances one can hear the
same—that on each occasion the one and the same work
should, if I may so state it, appear as its original self? With
several experiences of the same tree, the matter seems to us
easy to understand; perceptions of the tree differ one from
the other because they are subjective and therefore in each of
their phases differently constituted, but these perceptions
give us access to the *same* material object that exists by itself
in space and is not concerned with our experiences. Having
its own characteristics, the tree can, as it were, wait quietly in
space until someone notices it and learns something about it.
Even if no one is learning anything about it, that in no way
interferes with the tree's existence or affects the cluster of its
properties. This conclusion appears obvious even though it
has frequently caused philosophers many theoretical head-
aches. As for the musical work that is neither physical nor
mental (surely not a conscious experience or any part of it) as
the above naive view proclaims, how can it "await" our perceptions and manifest itself to us as exactly the same? Where
is that B Minor Sonata "lying in wait"? In the space of the
real world there are certainly no musical works when there is
no one to perform or hear them. And the specific performances of the sonata are not in any sense "objective" in contrast to the listening that is a conscious activity by certain
people. What then ensures us that despite differences in performance—assuming only that these performances are not
very inadequate—we hear the same sonata? The *same* and not
just one *like* it. Some philosophers accept the existence of

ideal objects, immutable and atemporal, having no origin and never ceasing to exist. The objects of mathematical investigations supposedly belong to this class. Are Chopin's B Minor Sonata and other musical works such "ideal" objects? We cannot agree to this, for who would deny that the sonata in question was created at a particular time by Chopin? Historians of music may even try to fix a reasonably accurate time when Chopin worked on the sonata and finished it. They say that Chopin's "legacy" included certain works, the sonata in question among them. So they must think it true that the B Minor Sonata has continued to exist and that Chopin's death has not in any way affected it. But how long it will continue to exist, whether eternally or for only a few years more, no one can predict. But the very fact that it came to be in the particular time is enough to reject the hypothesis that it is one among ideal objects, even assuming that we accept the existence of such objects.

To avoid such difficulties some perhaps will try to abandon presystematic convictions and once again seek refuge in a radically psychologistic view of the musical work. This view finds support in Husserl's critique of psychologism in logic wherein it was taken in many areas to be untenable to treat certain objects as mental facts or as a conscious experience or part of one. But it may be that in the realm of musical works things are different. Someone might say: is it not only a kind of illusion when it seems to us that we commune with the same work, with the same Chopin sonata? And is it not just an illusion that in listening to a certain performance of a given sonata we do not have the sense that the sonata was just coming into being and was ceasing to be at the end of its last chord? Or maybe this is not an illusion but only a certain false, theoretical idea to which we succumb under the influence of historical suggestions. For we know surely that Chopin has "written" that sonata, that it was published, and that this knowledge may lead us to the false conclusion that the sonata "exists." Yet perhaps no sonata by Chopin or any other musical work actually exists, but only particular performances. Perhaps we are also wrong in assuming, as we normally do, that all listeners at the same concert hear the same performance of a certain sonata. Is it not the case that when we exchange views at the end of the concert, we often reach the conclusion that there are considerable differences as to what each one of us has heard? Frequently we are unable to agree with regard to many details of performance, one of us valuing them highly, the other responding indifferently or even very critically. Should we then perhaps agree that there are simply specific subjective phenomena that are the performance of a certain sonata, differing partially or wholly from one listener to another, while both performances and that B Minor Sonata are just conventional linguistic fictions, useful in practical life but in reality devoid of existence? Subjective experience, subjective phenomena, are mental, but their acceptance causes no difficulties, for even materialists are inclined to accept the existence of mental phenomena and they deny only that this existence is separate from physical processes. The ultimate answer here does not concern us, for surely all we need to know is how to classify musical works. As such, they do not exist, while what does exist are certain processes of mental facts. Is this not the simplest solution and the most persuasive?

But if this solution were correct, there would be no sense in distinguishing the performances of a musical work from the work itself. Similarly there would be no justification for distinguishing a single performance from many other specific subjective phenomena experienced by this or that listener at the concert. We would then have no reason to talk about the identity of the musical work (that unique B Minor Sonata) or inquire into the conditions for the retention of that identity. This would not bother us: we should merely get rid of one theoretical headache. Unfortunately, however, we would have to abandon a range of judgments that—in the process of learning about music—we often proclaim as true. This would apply to our judgment that the B Minor Sonata consists of a specific number of movements, composed in particular keys, that for instance in the first movement there are particular subjects with a distinct harmonic framework that modulates in a particular way as the work progresses. These would all be false judgments since they would refer to a nonexistent object. It would be false also to claim, for instance, that the execution of the B Minor Sonata by a pianist at one concert was better than that by another performer at another concert, that one of them was faithful while the other departed from the original in many ways. These judgments would be not merely foolish but downright stupid. For what is the point of saying that one performance rather than another gives a more nearly accurate account of the B Minor Sonata when the sonata does not in fact exist and when there is nothing real with which these performances may be compared? Are we really going to agree that such judgments concerning the sonata itself and its performances are all false and stupid? If that which is to be "performed" does not exist, it would be senseless to invent the concept of "performance." Are we going to agree to this, too? As for the consequences of a psychologistic notion of a musical work, these go even further, leading to various grotesque assertions not worth citing here.

In the light of the difficulties outlined here, musical works now become puzzling objects—their essence and existence unclear—even though we have communed with them regularly as with good friends, and they have constituted a completely mundane and natural segment of our cultural world. Are not those commonsense presystematic convictions to be blamed for leading us this way? Should we not, therefore, critically examine these convictions and try to improve them or reject them altogether? Let us try.

1

The Musical Work and Its Performance

Which of the two possibilities then are we to accept: are we to agree that we need to distinguish the B Minor Sonata by Chopin from its many performances or alternatively that this distinction is not justified?

Looking more closely into the matter, we are led to the conviction that this distinction has to be regarded as proper, although at this stage we do not prejudge the question of whether we need to accept the *existence* of the musical work and its particular performances. For the moment we are suggesting only that a work and performances are not all one and the same, even should they all turn out to be merely a fiction.

The thesis that the musical work is not the same as its various performances is justified by the fact that certain valid judgments about specific performances turn out to be false with reference to the musical work itself (say, the B Minor Sonata by Chopin) and vice versa—that judgments seeming to be true of the sonata itself turn out to be false with reference to its specific performances. We can point to some features of performances of the sonata that do not belong to that sonata, and in turn to features of the sonata that do not belong to its performances. In asserting this, I am not prejudging the issue of whether the sonata, or its performances exist. I am claiming only that if something like that sonata were to exist, it would not possess all of those properties associated with its specific performances—should they exist—and vice versa. Thus:

1. Each performance of a certain musical work is a certain individual occurrence (process)[1] developing in time and placed in it univocally. A performance begins at a specific moment, lasts for a given and measurable period of time, and ends at a specific moment. As a process, every specific performance of a musical work can take place only once. When completed, the performance can neither continue nor repeat itself. It may be followed by another completely new performance in a different time span—different even if remarkably like the first performance—for example, a second playing of the same record on the same gramophone. Such a "repetition" of "the same" performance with the aid of a gramophone creates certain theoretical difficulties. We will disregard them here and confine ourselves to "live" performances. These differ not only in being placed at different times but also in many purely musical details even when the performer tries very hard to perform a particular work in the same way. The realization that doing so verges on the impossible prevents the finest artists from performing any particular work twice at the same concert and this especially so when the performance has been close to perfection.

2. Each performance of a musical work is above all an acoustic process. It is made up of a certain cluster of succeed-

---

1. There are three types of objects temporally determined: objects subsisting in time (things, people), processes (race, war, the development of an organism), and finally, events (someone's death, the start of a specific performance of the B Minor Sonata). These three types of temporally determined objects differ among themselves both as to the mode of their existence and their form, and with regard to their possible properties. I have discussed this fully in my *Does the World Exist?*, chapter 6 of volume 1, chapter 5, section 59, volume 2.

ing sound products caused by an almost contemporaneous process activated by the performer. This process is made up of complex physical acts (for example, fingers striking piano keys, the vibration and resonance of strings, the vibration of the air) and mental acts by the performer (as, for example, his consciousness of the acts he is performing, his control over them, his listening to his own performance and being affected by the composition).

3. Each performance is univocally fixed in space, both objectively and phenomenally—objectively in the sense that the produced sound waves expand in space from a particular point, embracing a defined area; phenomenally, in the sense that the sound products constituting a particular performance and developing as it progresses are perceived by the listeners as reaching them "from over there," "from the platform." We may get closer to these sounds or move further away within the concert hall and consequently hear the performance more or less satisfactorily—that is, more or less clearly, with a fuller or a dampened sound. All this is possible only because the performance of the work is given to us in space at a determined point in the form of sound products developing in time.

Whether, during this phenomenally localized performance of a work, the experience is confined to auditory perception or whether visual perceptions are also included (for we can see the movements of the performers) may be a matter of dispute. But this has no great significance for us because in each case the phenomenon of the localization in space of sound products constitutes the performance of the musical work.

4. Every performance of a musical work is given us as auditory, that is, in a certain multitude of auditory perceptions passing continuously, one into the other. Musically sounding products and processes (chords, melodies, and the

like belonging to the whole of a particular performance are given us as particular auditory objects because we experience the appropriate auditory aspects or auditory phenomena. This fact is generally overlooked by psychologists, who tend to treat auditory perception as simply the possession of a certain multitude of so-called auditory experiences that they identify with "sounds." On the whole, the commonly accepted psychological doctrines do not distinguish between an auditory object and an auditory aspect (gestalt) whose base is constituted by certain auditory experiential data. But closer analysis demonstrates that this distinction is necessary. Every note or acoustic product that sounds for even a brief period, and especially the performance of a musical work as a whole, possesses a multiplicity of auditory aspects enabling the listener to apprehend the given auditory product or to perform that work. These auditory aspects will vary with each listener and in successive phases of listening to the same note, melody, or chord. They would also differ within the same phase of a performance, were the listener able to hear a musical work from two different points in space. Because a performance can occur only once, it is not possible, without artificial aid, to hear the very same performance twice from two different points in space. Nevertheless, it is possible to change one's position during a performance, for example, by walking around the concert hall. One would then become conscious of how auditory aspects change. With artificial aids—for example, microphones spaced throughout the hall—it would be possible to experience simultaneously two different formations of auditory aspects during the same performance, for instance by listening with one ear directly and with the other through an earphone connected to a microphone. In this manner we could become conscious of contrast between the one performance and the different formations of auditory perceptions.

Other changes besides those of position are significant. Every change in the intensity and concentration of our auditory attention, every change in our emotional attitude, and many other kinds of changes have a profound influence upon the auditory aspects we are experiencing, while the properties of performance are not on the whole sensitive to such changes in the experienced aspects. On the other hand, such changes as take place in the *content* of the experienced auditory aspects, themselves dependent upon changes taking place in the base of the auditory experiential data and on the mode of the listeners' reaction to them, are all reflected in the concrete aspect of the performance objectively given us. This aspect we shall call a "concretion" of the work's performance. On the whole, we identify a concretion of a performance with the given performance. But hearing the same performance only twice (for example, on a gramophone record) can make us conscious of the difference between the concretion of a performance and the performance as such. As for changes taking place in experiencing aspects, which are manifested in the concretion of a performance, we may doubt whether the moments appearing consequentially as properties of the performance effectively do belong to it, or whether they are the direct consequence of the mode of listening, that is inter alia of the mode of experiencing auditory aspects—whether therefore they are characteristic of a given concretion. A performance may present itself to us as "blurred" or "sharp," but in discovering those characteristics, we may wonder whether they really existed or are to be attributed to our mode of listening at the moment. We need some controlling factor to decide this issue.

5. Specific performances of the same musical work by several interpreters, or even by the same interpreter, normally differ not only in their individuality, their position in space and time, but also their various qualitative properties

such as tonal colorings, tempi, dynamic detail, the perspicuity of specific subjects, and so on. So long as the performer is a live human being, it is impossible to eradicate these differences completely, however he or she might try. Moreover, a direct perception of a work and a purely mechanical reproduction of a particular performance would always differ in that the experience would afford concrete temporal coloring of the performance heard in the specific time, and there might be other immediately perceived differences as well. How a particular performance is given us in direct perception depends not only on objective conditions but also on subjective conditions which change from occasion to occasion. The influence of these upon the concrete manifestations of the heard performance can never be fully eliminated. This applies to the purely auditory properties of a performance but also in a much stronger sense to a variety of nonacoustic elements structuring themselves over the acoustic material, and, for the performance of the musical work, as significant as the purely acoustic properties—for instance, a more or less clearly defined melodic line, emotional coloring, and the like. Such factors determine the specificity of particular concretions of the same performance of a musical work.

6. Every specific performance of a musical work is an individual object, in every respect univocally, positively determined in the long run by the qualities of the smallest possible variation—these being incapable of any further differentiation.

So much for certain properties of performance of a musical work. If we attempt now to apply these assertions to the musical work itself, as manifested to us concretely in specific performances, then (although our knowledge of the work of music is not yet clarified and grounded in detailed analysis) we are soon convinced that these assertions are not true of the musical work and that in their place we have to accept other assertions that in turn are not true of the performances. But we need to remember that we are discussing the completed work of music and that all problems relating to the processes of its coming into being in the creative acts of the composer are beyond the confines of this discussion. Our analyses of the musical work will confirm the assertions which I list as follows:

1.   Every musical work is an object persisting in time. (I shall return to the question of whether in some sense one may ascribe to it the structure of a process.) Having come into existence at a certain moment, it exists as the same product even though the processes through which it came into being have passed. Thus, as I have already remarked, one cannot, as W. Conrad once claimed, regard the musical work as an ideal object.[2] Such a possibility is ruled out by the fact that the work arises in time, a fact surely beyond dispute. On a contrary view, one would need to regard a composer's creative processes in principle as the same as those taking place in the listener when he becomes acquainted with a finished work.

From the assertion that a work of music is not an ideal object, it does not follow that it is a real object, since the domains of those two concepts do not cover all objects. Even the assertion that a work of music is an object enduring in time is not equivalent to the assertion that it is a real object. The question of existence, and in particular of the mode of existence of a musical work, must be left in abeyance until we obtain more precise results from analytical investigations of the musical work.

---

2. W. Conrad, *Der ästhetische Gegenstand,* "Zeitschrift für Ästhetik," volumes 3 and 4.

Although a musical work is an object enduring in time, it is not "temporal" in the same sense as its specific performances. As I have already asserted, while the performances are processes, the musical work as such is not a process. While the movements of a performed work of music succeed each other in specific, successive, temporal phases, all the movements of the musical work itself exist together in a completed whole. If, despite this, the parts of a completed work display a certain specific order of succession, and even if, as we shall see, a certain quasi-temporal structure is immanent in every musical work (this I shall fully clarify below), it does not follow at all that a musical work does not possess all its parts simultaneously or that some of its parts are temporally earlier than others. Similarly, from the fact that the values of a mathematical series (for instance the geometrical one) are ordered in a particular way and may on account of this ordering be numbered, it does not follow that a geometric series in a mathematical sense is extended in time and is a process in the state of becoming.[3] These assertions, however, require a deeper justification that we shall only be able to provide later.

On the other hand, each individual performance of a musical work effectively spreads itself in time in such a way that its separate parts unfold in different time spans, and, in turn, parts of those parts gradually manifest themselves in constantly new time-phases inevitably receding into the past. Having receded, they cease to exist, they sink into the past, from which—if one may so put it—they never return, but rather sink into it more deeply, becoming more and more distant from the ever-renewing present. Furthermore, the

---

3. I have here in mind mathematic series for which there exists a general formula of variables, for instance $K_n = aq^{n-1}$. My assertion in the text does not apply to the so-called *wahlfreie Folgen,* which were pointed out by the intuitionists (Brouwer and others).

particular performances differ in their duration: some faster, some slower, and in the framework of this process the tempo of their development varies (assuming we are not confronted with a precisely regulated mechanical reproduction, one which, precisely because of the monotony of its evolution in time, creates a negative aesthetic impression).

With reference to the work itself, none of this makes any sense. The work has the one and only order of succession of its parts, a unique quasi-temporal structure determined once and for all by its author. This structure includes the determined tempi that are quite independent of the phases of concretely experienced qualitative time, and especially the phases of time in which one or other of its performances takes place.[4] Specific performances constitute more or less clear deviations from the fixed quasi-temporal structure, as if "foreseen" in the work itself, even though the performer on the whole tries to recreate in his performance just this quasi-temporal structure that characterizes the work. It is for him a model and a measure.

2. No musical work is conditioned in its creation and continued existence by those real processes that produce its particular performances, say, the action of the fingers upon the keyboard. The causes of its coming to be are quite different psychophysical events, the artist's creative processes, which in any case need not express themselves in an actual performance on a particular instrument. On the other hand,

---

4. I stumbled on this "order of succession" of the parts of the work and its quasi-temporal structure when I was analyzing the literary work in my *The Literary Work of Art* (1931), of which this work originally constituted a section. What I had to say there, together with later analysis in my *Cognition of the Literary Work* (1937), may be extended to cover the musical work and also works of film. The first to notice this structure was not Lessing, as one would expect, but Herder. Later no one took much notice of this problem, and what we do find in Herder is no more than an initial intuition.

the processes that produce the specific performances of the work do not produce the work itself: their purpose is to enable one to hear *in concreto* the work through the performance. Given the appropriate expertise and musical imagination, one can become acquainted with a work without the aid of a performance by simply reading the score, although one cannot in this manner attain the fullness and concretion of acquaintance that are possible when attending a performance. Once the processes that bring the performance about come to an end, the performance itself ceases to exist. Should the processes be interrupted, the performance too is interrupted. It can be resumed after the interval, but this break will remain in it forever, thus making impossible an aesthetically satisfying perception of the work. That is why whenever performers are forced to interrupt a performance they do not resume it but start again at the beginning. None of these assertions can be applied to the work of music itself, and any such attempt results in absurdity.

3. In contrast to its specific performances the work of music possesses no defined spatial localization. No such localization is specified either by the creative acts of the composer or by the score. Thus the work may be performed anywhere, and any spatial location of the performance inevitably tied to it is each time different and has no significance for an aesthetic perception of the work. In listening to the performance we must ignore this aspect.

4. It is not true that any specific musical work, for instance Beethoven's Fifth Symphony, manifests itself immediately in the varying auditory aspects experienced by the listener, and that, as a consequence, the work itself assumes a variety of the successive properties and characteristics evidenced in specific performances. The work remains insensible to the processes occurring in the contents and in the manner of experiencing auditory aspects of particular per-

formances: it does not change as a result of the performances, acquiring this or that characteristic for the reason described above. Assuredly it is true that when a specific perform-ance—as a result of bad acoustics in the hall or undue dis-tance from the performance—seems blurred or lacking in tone, this makes difficult an aesthetic perception of the work itself and may even, in borderline cases, make it impossible. But as a consequence, no one would assert that the work itself has become blurred or flat and empty in tone. These factors cannot make it change at all. No work is a *hic et nunc* developing acoustic phenomenon, as it would have to be to undergo change resulting from variations in the range of au-ditory aspects randomly developing in particular listeners. Were we to agree that the work is thus affected, at the same time we would have to agree that it possesses mutually ex-clusive properties: that it is both what it would have to be as a consequence of acquiring certain properties in one perform-ance, and also what it would have to be with properties flow-ing from other performances given us through experience of other aspects. This too appears glaringly false with reference to the musical work itself, nor is it, so to speak, pure theory. The matter has consequences in musical practice.

So long as we are not completely naive listeners, we try, when listening to a particular performance of, say, Beetho-ven's Fifth Symphony, to ignore all those objectively given details of the actual performance which appear in it as a con-sequence of the chance circumstances in which our listening occurs—circumstances which have their influence on the concrete content of the auditory aspects we are experiencing and which affect the concretion of the heard performance. We thus perform a certain selection. With regard to the con-cretely appearing properties of the performance, we ascribe some of them to the work itself that we are attempting to hear and extrapolate from the concrete whole of the performance. We ignore others, ascribing them to the chance character either of the performance or of the listening—in other words, of the contents and mode of experiencing the auditory aspects. The process of listening to a musical work is, as it develops, much more complex than it first appears, while on the other hand just that complexity—as well as various concrete details which characterize it and which I cannot here discuss—constitutes one of the arguments for the differentiation between the work of music, its performance, and its concretion.

If between the musical work and the multiplicities of auditory aspects (by experiencing which the listener is able to hear the performance and through it to grasp the work itself) there is a connection, it is only that every musical work determines a certain ideal system of auditory aspects to be experienced by a listener if the work is to be given faithfully and fully in aesthetic experience. The work's own structure and qualitative properties will, for instance, indicate that it has to be heard—within feasible limits—from a certain distance, thereby designating also the types of ideally determined auditory aspects. If someone, for instance, wished to listen to Chopin's Prelude No. 6 from a distance of one kilometer, we would have to tell him that he is as little aware of the work's properties as the person who, in a snobbish desire to be seen, insists on the front row at a performance of Beethoven's Ninth Symphony.

But the fact that there occurs this kind of congruence between the musical work and ideal systems of auditory aspects does not prove that the musical work manifests itself directly or immediately through the auditory aspects.

5. In contrast to the multiplicity of its possible performances, every specific musical work, like Beethoven's Ninth Symphony, is absolutely unique. This at once rules out its identity with the performances. In consequence, it lies outside all those differences that necessarily occur between par-

ticular performances. Or to put it another way: just because these sorts of differences cannot appear in the musical work itself (and the very thought appears absurd) it is clear that the work is not identical with its performances and is an individual, while any number of performances of it are possible. What sense would it make to claim, for instance, that the Andante of Beethoven's *Pathétique Sonata* has two different tempi simultaneously, that it has contrasting dynamics or contrasting tonal colorings? If a particular performance contains tempi, dynamics, and melodic lines differing from those proper to the work, this is simply a false performance. When we listen to it, either we cannot perceive the work aesthetically at all or we simply disregard the performance's faulty qualities and imagine in their place properties that do belong to the work. We then deplore the performance as false—too fast, lack-luster, too loud, soulless and so on. As we have argued, the performance has to be apart from the work, if the given work is to be faithfully represented, if it is to appear in all its glory. Should we say sometimes of the work itself that it is too colorless, too monotonous, or too loud, we are here not dealing with a relationship between the actual performance and something differing from it, to be recreated and in its own self revealed, but rather the relationship between certain characteristics or parts of the work itself and the aesthetic value that it claims as a work of art. The relationship here may also be between certain characteristics of the work and other properties it would have acquired but for certain of its shortcomings, and these—with the help of the above critical terms, we wish to single out—for example, if the work were not as monotonous as in fact it is. On the other hand, when we refer to a certain performance as being too fast or too monotonous, we cannot apply these terms to the work itself since they arise from a comparison between the performance and the work.

6. One may legitimately doubt whether a musical work

is in every respect univocally and ultimately determined by its "lowest" properties that cannot be further differentiated. Resolution of this problem depends on whether the work of music has to be identified with (1) the product exclusively determined by the score, or (2) the product that is equivalent to adequate aesthetic perception. We shall take up this issue later. For the moment we may observe that in the first instance we would have to accept that a musical work contains features such that it is not univocally determined by qualities incapable of further differentiation. This applies for example to the tonal coloring which forms part of the work. The score prescribes simply the kind of instrument on which the work is to be performed, therefore indirectly determining the type of tonal coloring, but not the lowest variant of that type, that absolutely individual coloring which is realized only in a certain performance. The same applies to the fullness of tones or sounds that is strictly connected with the tonal coloring. To a certain extent the same problem arises with reference to the absolute pitch of the notes. Although it would be possible by physical means to define with great precision the absolute pitches of sounds appearing in a certain work, as we soon realize, we are not particularly bothered by this. Small differences in the absolute pitch of notes are of no great consequence for the musical work. Undoubtedly if anyone wished to play the Funeral March in Chopin's B Minor Sonata in a high register, or to sing Elsa's part in *Lohengrin* in a deep bass, he would frustrate the perception of these works through such performances. But tiny shifts by a fraction of a tone are not significant.

It appears that in this respect the musical work is not as rigorously defined as one would think. In his above-mentioned work, Conrad talks of the *Irrelevanzsphären* of a musical work in the realm of which differences between specific performances of the work are of no consequence. Indeed, he is right. There is a "sphere of irrelevance" within musical works and perhaps in all works of art. But Conrad does not say why it is possible for such a sphere to exist and be different for every work. It appears that this is possible only when the work itself is not in every respect univocally determined by the lowest qualities. To this matter I shall return.

If, on the other hand, we were to take the musical work to be exactly as it appears in a concrete but adequate aesthetic perception (the difficulty here would be a proper definition of adequacy) then we would be justified in doubting whether it is in some respects undetermined. To this matter too I shall have to return but I mention it now to indicate that these sorts of problems do not arise with reference to a specific performance of a musical work, and also to signal that the term "musical work" is ambiguous and requires stricter definition.

All the facts I have cited above force us to admit that a musical work is indeed something radically different from all its possible performances, even though there are naturally many similarities between them. It is because these similarities occur that we can speak of performances of a certain, determined work. Later we shall see what this assertion means for the problem of the existence, the mode of existence, and the identity of a musical work. For the time being we have to consider the following two questions:

1. whether a musical work is identical with certain conscious experiences of the composer or of the listener;
2. whether the work of music is identical with its score. Only when we are able to discard both these possibilities, will the question of the essence of a musical work reveal itself to us in its proper form.

2

The Musical Work
and Conscious Experiences

We are living through the aftermath of psychologism, which still has many followers, particularly in Poland, although elsewhere its grip has been broken and it is seen as a thing of the past.[1] Especially to art theorists and musicologists, who themselves take no interest in philosophy yet are inclined to make general assertions regarding the objects of their investigations, it seems almost obvious that a work of art, and especially a musical work, is something "mental": a cluster of imaginings or auditory experiences. I can almost hear some of my readers saying: why does the author complicate a simple matter? A musical work is above all a certain cluster of sounds with which one associates feelings, thoughts, and imaginings. And, as we learn from physicists and psychologists, sounds are nothing but sense-experiences and therefore mental experiences. The same applies to presentations, feelings, and so-called presentational judgments.

It is therefore clear that the musical work is something mental. And it follows that no single musical work is the same for several different mental subjects, or for the same subject listening to a second performance of "the same"

---

1. Psychologism, that is, the treatment as mental facts (or as conscious experiences) of objects that in their nature are not mental, finds support most readily among people without philosophical understanding who, nevertheless, think they need to proclaim philosophical views in order to impress others with their learning.

work. All we have are conscious experiences: on the one hand, experiences while composing a given work and, on the other, experiences of listeners whose nerve-endings are stimulated by sound waves produced by the vibrations of an instrument being played. Whatever the composer experienced is long past, and we can conjecture it only on the basis of our own reactions in the course of listening. Strictly speaking, there is nothing more than a growing cluster of experiences resembling each other in their response to similar physical stimuli—the sound waves. When, in common speech, we talk as if there existed a single musical work (for example, Szymanowski's Fourth Symphony) we are expressing ourselves imprecisely, yielding either to certain linguistic suggestions and fictions or to a usage convenient in daily life. But we must not yield to such imprecisions when conducting theoretical investigations. Acknowledging the results of scientific investigations, we know that physics and psychology have clarified this issue: a musical work is obviously a selection of mental facts conditioned by physical stimuli. The problem of identity of a musical work arises from the illusions created by the imprecisions of ordinary language. The scientific task is to describe and explain causally the experiences we undergo while listening to a certain musical work.

Unravelling the assumptions hidden in psychologistic notions of art—especially music—would take us too far. Let us confine ourselves to an attempt to acquire the experience of objects that we wish to study and to remain faithful to the data of this experience, accommodating to them the sense of our assertions and not falsifying these assertions even in the name of the most "scientific" theorists within certain philosophical movements—here I have chiefly in mind the positivists and the neopositivists. Let us inquire whether it is possible to accept the foregoing view of a musical work.

First of all, we need to reach an understanding of the term "mental." What in fact do psychologistic theorists mean when they claim that a musical work is "mental"? This seems to mean that the work is a conscious human experience or a purposefully selected cluster of such experiences, among which the most important role is played by so-called auditory experiences. When we ask what leads psychologistic theorists to such an assertion, we find that it is the acceptance of another concept related to the mental. According to this concept, "the mental" covers everything that is neither physical nor existing independent of conscious experiences. Such matters are called "subjective," and the subjective is imperceptibly identified with experience or its constituent parts. Only the material is regarded as having independent existence.

On one point we can agree at once: a musical product is not existentially independent of its composer's conscious experiences. It may be that it is not even fully existentially independent of its listeners' conscious experiences. If we were therefore to agree to the above sense of the term "subjective"—without identifying that which is "subjective" in this sense with a conscious experience or its constituent parts— then we would have to acknowledge that in this sense a musical work is "subjective." Still, on this basis there is no reason to assert that it is something mental or an element in some conscious experience. Further, if we were to accept the assertion of critical realism, according to which all qualitative products (among others, sounds and tonal structures we perceive in the outside world) are "only subjective" (a matter for far-reaching doubts even though the whole of contemporary physics is written in this spirit), "objective" existence may here be ascribed only to waves from material fields of force. Even then it would not be possible to claim that a musical work is a conscious experience or its constituent elements. Arguing against this assertion is the very fact that all experiences and their elements are accessible to cognition only in acts of "reflection," i.e., inner experience, and that no one cognizes musical work in these kinds of acts. Also, surely all will agree that a musical work is not an act of consciousness, that is, an act of listening or imagining. Even the psychologizing theorists would reject such an interpretation of their position. Were we to agree on the "subjectivity" of musical works in the above-mentioned sense, we would at the same time have to reject the assertion that these works are conscious experiences or their constituent parts, since experiences in this sense are not "subjective." This is so because experiences are not existentially dependent upon other experiences—for instance, the acts of "reflection" directed upon them.

Perhaps the psychologizing theorists would say that the music work is the *content* of the composer's experiences during composition or those of the listeners during one of the performances. Unfortunately, the term "content of experience" is ambiguous when used by psychologists, and in this generally undetected ambiguity lies the apparent strength of the psychologistic theorists' notion. They often avoid criticisms by moving imperceptibly from one meaning to another. They also understand "content" so widely that everything which is neither an act of consciousness nor a material object becomes the "content" of a conscious experience. Such a definition precludes response, for in this sense "content" *ex definitione* may refer equally to a musical work or to any sensibly perceived object, taken precisely as perceived. But this extension of reference for the concept "content" is an abuse of language: the concept explains nothing, but with its aid nothing can be denied. We must, therefore, begin by establishing a useful meaning of this term. Since, however, in the case of a musical work we can only be concerned with

auditory perceptions or experiences that have their psychological base in these experiences, we may ask what one ought
to understand by the "content" of these experiences. Our
attitude toward a musical work may be purely intellectual—
if for instance, without listening to any performance we try
to understand or pass judgment on a work. While listening
to a musical work, we do experience a variety of feelings.
But if we could demonstrate that a musical work, independent of what it is like, differs from even these directly given
contents of perception or auditory imagining, then a fortiori
this would have had to be true in relation to all other conscious experiences here taken into consideration.

Let us then affirm that if "content" is really to be something mental in the sense of an experience of consciousness,
it must form an element, an effective part of that experience
and that part which we apprehend in the experience, yet not
form part of the experiencing itself. This is because the experiencing and all its elements form a conscious act, and we
have already agreed that the act is not under consideration.
The element we seek from an experience cannot at the same
time be something to which our experience refers, given us
while the experience is taking place, since this constitutes the
object of experience. What then in auditory perception does
constitute the effective element of our listening experience?

It is not easy to answer this question if our answer is to
give a faithful account of the facts, neither oversimplifying
them nor replacing them with something totally alien. In
our discussion, however, the theoretical situation is sim-
plified to the extent that the supporters of psychologism have
a ready answer as to what constitutes the content of auditory
perception. They will reply: it is simple—that which constitutes an effective element of auditory perception is none
other than the sensible auditory experience; just as, they will
add, the content of visual perceptions is visual experience,

and the content of tactile perception is tactile experience. In this manner everything would be settled and the supporters of psychologism would be convinced that this answer constituted the final clarification of the problem, if (a) there were absolutely no doubts about the meaning of auditory, visual, and other "experiences," and (b) we were certain that what we had in mind was undoubtedly an effective part of an experience of a perception—be it auditory, visual, or any other kind.

Unfortunately, even though "sense experiences" have been discussed in European philosophy for several hundred years and for the last ninety years, beginning with Fechner, they have been studied by experimental psychologists, neither of these problems has been finally settled. We cannot, for instance, use the concept of "element" in Mach's sense, because this concept as introduced and used in his *Analyse der Empfindungen* is ambiguous. It is true that since Mach's day the discussion of this matter has progressed (though professional psychologists working experimentally have made only a small contribution), particularly in the work of Bergson and the phenomenologists Husserl, Schapp, Hofmann, and Conrad-Martius. But if I were to refer to these views even in passing, my investigation into the musical work would turn into an analysis of the structure and process of sense-experience. It will perhaps be enough to say that the so-called perceptions are neither objects given us in sense-experience nor their directly given qualitative characteristics, but rather certain qualitative data that we experience when we are objectively given things or other objects that have been qualitatively determined. In particular, auditory "perceptions" are not sounds, tones, chords, or melodies, or even their qualitative characteristics such as pitch or coloring, the harmonic quality of a chord, or the shape of a melody. Tones, chords, and melodies are given us in simple auditory experience as

objects, for instance, as constituents of an individual performance. In perceiving them, however, we experience particular data that, being fluid, pass into one another. These
have qualities that are impossible to describe directly (without turning them into objects) but that, speaking generally,
are somehow related in their general character to the qualities
appearing within the confines of auditorily perceived objects. We require a special cognitive act, a special kind of
"reflection," in order to apprehend them without falsifying
their specific characteristics and mode of existence. When we
achieve this "reflection," without at the same time ceasing to
perceive the performance of a certain musical work developing in time, we become persuaded that the sound products,
which form part of the performance (and even more the performance itself), are radically different from the auditory experiential data. We become persuaded that they go beyond
such data, even the simplest of whose qualitative characteristics manifest themselves solely through a fluid mass of multiple experiential data or auditory aspects constructed upon
them. A sound or a note that we hear for even a brief moment
(e.g., one second) is given us as one and the same (an enduring
sound continuum), while the experiential data are constantly
new, changeable in their saturation (the intensity of their
manifestations) in the way they come, by the constant variety
of their qualities, to dominate or recede from the field of our
experiences. The data that have just been present pass away
and are succeeded by new ones; but a note or a chord sounding through time (even though its initial sound has passed)
remains the same and is so perceived. The chord does not
consist, as some naively think, of experiential data, nor are its
characteristics identical with such data. It manifests itself as a
totally new being in relation to them. Thus, even the simplest
sound within a concrete, individual performance of a musical
work does not constitute any effective part of the multiplicity

of the auditory experiential data. Even if we were to include such data among the elements of the perceptual experience — and this inclusion is, as I remarked, a matter of dispute—even then the sound products forming part of the performance would not constitute any part of that experience and in that sense would be in transcendent relation to it. This does not prevent their being palpably given to us.

Ignoring the question of how it happens that in experiencing the fluid data of auditory experiences we notice tonal products, from which the performance of the musical work is constructed, we can assert only that proper correlations do take place between the multiplicities of experiential data and sound products forming part of the performance. If we are to perceive certain determined sound products, then in the realm of our auditory experiential data there must appear multiplicities of sound products that in a determined way either follow each other or appear contemporaneously, and vice versa. If we experience certain multiplicities of auditory experiential data, as a consequence there must appear among the objects we hear (sounds, notes, chords, and melodies) certain fully determined products with univocally determined properties. Despite the work of C. Stumpf, these correlations in the realm of auditory perception have not been developed in detail. Concerning visual perception, relationships have been worked out much more fully. It remains a fact that these are correlations of only two mutually exclusive realms. In other words: if the data of auditory perception constitute the content of auditorily perceived experiences, then the sounds, tones, chords, and melodic products that we perceive objectively are not the content of auditorily perceived experiences, and therefore, a fortiori, are not the content of any conscious experiences.

Even more so, no sound product of a higher order, for example, a certain determined melody woven into an ac-

companiment and taken in the individual fullness of its concrete performance, constitutes the content of any conscious
experience. When we perceive the melody auditorily, we experience, on the one hand, a multiplicity of fluid experiential
data, and the auditory aspects constructed upon them. On
the other hand, our act of perception contains a determined
intention relating to that melody—an intention that I designate, and not the immediately present content of the act of
perception. This intention belongs of course to consciousness. Given a certain mode of understanding the "mental," it
can be concluded that the intention is mental, but it, too,
differs radically from the heard melody. It does not have the
properties possessed by the melody, and it can come to be
known in a totally different way from a melody: that is to
say, it can be given in an immanent, reflective perception
(not by any definition a sense-experience) while the individual melody now occurring is given objectively in a non-
reflective, outer sense-experience, that is, in one which
makes use of the content or data we are experiencing. The
same may be said about all elements and dependent moments in an individual performance of any work of music.
They are all objects or objective moments to which our act
of auditory perception refers, but they are not in any sense
the content of the auditory perception. The same can be said
about these objects or objective moments in relation to all
experiences, be they acts of understanding a concrete performance constructed on the immediate auditory perception
or acts of feelings entwining with the aura of their qualities
given us in perception as performance of a particular work.
This holds true also in relation to all experiences in which
only indirectly (without hearing) we refer to a particular performance (for instance discussing with friends after a concert
the detail of Chopin's B Minor Sonata).

Thus one individual performance of a musical work forms no part of conscious experiences and consequently is not in any sense mental. Only a primitive understanding of mental or conscious experiences, on the one hand, and of the performnce of musical works, on the other, could support this notion, in essence absurd, that the performance of a musical work is mental in character. A fortiori this applies to the musical work, to Chopin's B Minor Sonata, which, as one and the same, manifests itself to us through a variety of performances, and—as we have shown—is radically different from its various performances and forms no element of them. In relation to the experience of perception, wherein one of its performances is given us, the musical work as such is transcendent at an even higher level than the individual performance: we have here something like a transcendence of a second order ("transcend" has many meanings. Here it means simply "stepping beyond conscious experiences and their elements"). This in itself establishes the fact that the work of music (a certain determinate one like Chopin's B Minor Sonata) is neither mental nor subjective, that is, belonging to the elements or moments of the perceiving subject.

3

The Musical Work and Its Score

Having rejected attempts to identify the musical work with its performance or with certain conscious experiences, we now have to consider the supposition that the musical work is nothing but its notation or score. This thought will undoubtedly occur to those investigators who regard the postulate *entia non sunt multiplicanda praeter necessitatem* as an overriding principle—that is, to reduce all types of objects to material things or processes or at worst to certain mental processes. When dealing with objects that others maintain cannot be reduced to the material or the mental, such investigators talk of so-called metaphysical hypostases, regarding these as a grave methodological error. Admittedly the notion of "reduction" has not been fully clarified, but the positivists do not like to acknowledge this, since such reduction often disagrees glaringly with positivism's chief postulate, namely, that one must simply acknowledge all "positive" data of experience. But they themselves unfortunately do not abide by this postulate.

There is only one sense in which I find comprehensible the reduction of a musical work to its score, namely, that the work of music and its score are identical and that in a concrete, individual case (say, that of Szymanowski's Fourth Symphony) we cannot discover, therefore, any characteristic of the musical work that is not also a characteristic of its score and vice versa—we can find no characteristics in the score that are not present in the given work. If, by the way, this issue were to be resolved in favor of identifying the musical work with its score, it would not, as we shall see, lead to the conclusion that a musical work is physical. This, however, is precisely the secret expectation of those who seek the reduction of a musical work to its score.

It is not, however, possible to bring about the identification of a musical work with its score. Neopositivists committed to so-called physicalism and intent upon avoiding the question of what a musical score (notation) actually is would probably say that the score or the notation is nothing but a sheet of paper with blobs of printer's ink spread on its surface in a particular, determined way. The manner of spacing that ink on the paper is the result of an agreement between the composers, the printers, and the readers of the score. In consequence one would have to admit that the score of Szymanowski's Fourth Symphony exists in as many copies as have so far been printed, a number that increases with every new printing. We would also have to agree that the score's properties include the chemical constituents of the paper and printer's ink as well as such developments as the ink's changing color when exposed to the sun. In their radicalism, the neopositivistic physicalists would undoubtedly not have balked at such assertions, although no one who is unprejudiced would agree to ascribe such properties to the score.[1] Perhaps the physicalists would have responded that there is no need to accept such consequences regarding the assertion about the identity of the score with a certain physical object, because in order to escape "metaphysical hypostases" it is

---

1. A reminder that I was writing these investigations at a time when physicalist tendencies were still very strong, both in the Vienna Circle and among some Polish philosophers. After the Prague Congress these tendencies subsided markedly.

sufficient to accept that the score is only a system of selected properties or is a determined part of the printed paper,
namely the system of conventionally agreed-upon colored
shapes on paper. Neither this nor other proposals, however,
save the physicalists' interpretation of the score. The decisive
factor is that were the score only a piece of printed paper, its
part, or a certain selection of its properties, it could not perform the function that, in fact, turns it into the score of a
particular musical work, namely, the function of *symbolizing*
certain determined objects or processes.

That which we call a printed "sign"—in particular a musical sign—is not just a blob of ink on paper or on some
other material substance. A material object as such cannot,
in the strict sense of the word, possess any immaterial properties or perform any immaterial function.[2] It can only be a
subject or a co-participator in physical processes, but these
do not include the function either of designating or of meaning, more precisely, of possessing meaning. Designating
functions are intentional, imposed upon the sign by a particular operation of consciousness performed by a certain conscious subject. No physical object (a chalk mark, a desk, a
lamp, etc.) can either designate on its own account or effectively acquire a designation through the act of a certain subject. A physical object (a lamp, a desk, a drawing) can only
be an ontic base of a sign, which itself is the product of a
subjective conscious operation that grants it just such an intentional function: for example, a certain typical visual shape
or color (as in the case of traffic lights). In other words, that
which is normally called the physical side of a sign is not a
physical object (a material thing) but only a certain typical

---

2. This of course is only true if among material properties we do not
include any possible dependent property. See my *Does the World Exist?*,
volume 2, section 55.

aspect—be it visual or auditory—that, thanks to an appropriate intentional supposition by the mental subject, appears to that subject palpably on the base of a material object of suitable material shape.

Within certain boundaries that do not entail a change in or disappearance of that typical aspect palpably manifesting itself on the base of a material object, that object can undergo determined changes. The so-called letters of the alphabet may be physically larger or smaller, a railway signal more or less covered in grime, and so on, but as long as the conventionally agreed-upon aspects may still appear palpably on the basis of the real objects despite these variations, then the sign remains the same and performs the same function of designating. For it is only the identically appearing *typical aspect* that performs the function of a sign: it bears the intentionally ascribed intention directed upon a certain defined object, process, or state of affairs. Given the railway conventions, a raised semaphore indicates that the way is clear.

The score is a system of signs of a particular kind. They are not physical although they appear on the base of certain physical things: for instance on sheets of paper suitably overprinted. These same signs appear on many different sheets of paper that form part of different copies in a given edition of the same score. Thus, identifying a musical work with its score cannot free us from accepting certain objects which are both immaterial and nonmental. The score itself is not mental: the signs we create by means of appropriate subjective operations are transcendent products in relation to these operations. In relation to the acts of understanding the signs, they are the transcendent objects. Exactly the same sign or arrangement of signs, as in a score, may constitute the object of many various acts of understanding and may be used for designating a certain object, irrespective of whether these acts are performed by one or several subjects. A sign is just the intersubjective means of communication regarding the objects designated. Notation has been invented so that various people might use it to play the same musical work. At this point, it becomes clear that it is impossible to identify the musical work with the score employed for various performances of that work.

The following reasons testify to this:

1. Not every musical work has been notated. Folk songs existed at a time when notation was unknown. Many composers simply improvised their works without ever notating them. This had no bearing on the creation of these works and only constituted a certain difficulty for repeat performances, since it is not easy to remember a work brought about by improvization. Whether works that arose in improvization and have not been notated or remembered by anyone still exist after a single performance is doubtful and difficult to decide. But the source of this difficulty resides in other facts that do not affect the difference between a musical work and the score by which it is notated.

2. A score consists of an arrangement of "imperative" symbols, which we fix with the help of various technical means—for instance with the aid of musical notation on paper or with the aid of a tape-recording. Strictly speaking, this fixing consists of endowing real objects with certain qualities, for example, the same repeated blobs of ink on paper enabling the reader to see in the blobs always the same symbols (signs) regarding which there is an intersubjective agreement that they always do mean the same thing. There is, of course, a large number of such systems of signs conventionally determined, and one must know the convention to be able to employ them accurately. But once we have learned the convention, our simple noticing of blobs on paper leads us to grasp the symbols themselves (the particular

musical notes) and with their aid to turn to what they designate. Every musical note univocally determines the pitch
and duration of a particular sound. The manner in which the
notes are disposed in relation to each other, again according
to certain conventions, informs us how certain notes either
co-exist or follow one another. Apart from the notation itself
there is additional information, usually supplied in ordinary
language, regarding the tonal coloring, the range of dynamics, the speed and rhythmical characteristics of the work.
The score thus designates what the work is to be like. But the
role of the score does not end here. It also constitutes an arrangement of *instructions* as to how to proceed in order to
achieve a faithful performance of a given work. In this double
sense a score consists of "imperative" symbols. The score,
finally, is a way of revealing the composer's wishes as to what
the work is to be like.

To the same extent that a sign is different from the object
it designates, a score is different from the musical work that
is designated by it. The ontic connection between the work
and the score consists only in a correlation created conventionally. Nor is this correlation in every respect isomorphic;
the same work may be "inscribed" within different nota-
tional systems; also, the work is not univocally in every respect defined in its properties by the score. The work possesses characteristics that do not pertain to the score and vice
versa. The work of music includes sounds, or strictly speaking, tonal qualitative aspects, melodic qualities, and qualitative characteristics of various kinds of harmony and disharmony (in the original, proper meaning of the word). None
of this forms part of the score nor characterizes it. The work
is determined by various rhythmic and dynamic properties
that it would make no sense to look for in the score. In contrast to a literary work, in which language organized in its

two-stratum structure forms a part, so that the work cannot even be perceived without its linguistic double strata, the relationship between a musical work and its score is much looser and more distant. Not only can a work of music in principle be heard without the aid of the score—we do not usually "read" musical works, though this of course does happen when we learn to play a particular work—but when we hear the work and perceive it aesthetically in the fullness of its properties and complete concretion, the score remains totally outside the work's range. Even those who know the score do not include it within the work's boundaries. Thus, the score not only is different from the musical work but also does not form any part of it and does not form any of its layers (assuming that talk of strata with reference to a musical work were at all acceptable). This does not contradict the fact that a musical work is intentionally designated by the score in cases where the score exists and that the score itself is intentionally designated by the composer's creative acts, so that ultimately the musical work has its source of existence and its properties in these acts. Where the composer has not notated his work, however, has not fixed it in a score, the work is derived directly from his creative intentional acts, intentions that are sometimes immediately realized in a performance by the composer himself.

4

Some Features of a Musical Work

If we agree about the foregoing distinctions, then the question becomes even more pressing as to what a musical work really is. The following sketchy analysis of its structure and properties provides groundwork for the solution of this problem.

But first, one more small point. There are many theories regarding the work of music, and it is quite difficult to decide which is true when we compare them with one another and subject them to dialectical treatment. What is more, the theories constitute not only specific formulations but also programmatic assertions. They express the aspirations of certain artists or at least of people whose interest in the theory of music is closely tied to their creative or performative practice. The theories constitute types of postulates as to what kinds of works are to be composed if they are to qualify as musical works. Consequently, composers attempt to realize these postulates in their works, thereby lending support to the theories. In contemporary European music this has led to great variety, so that it is extremely difficult to formulate a theory of musical composition to satisfy all trends and also to reveal a structure or a cluster of properties common to all these works. The contradictions between the various theories are for me less significant, because they are not on the whole concerned with the essential question of what the musical work really is but with the question of what properties a musical work should possess, according to a particular artistic program, for it is to be valuable as a work of art. This is a different problem, arising at a much later stage, since bad musical works are also the products of artistic activity, however faulty, and are musical works even though they not only lack value but may be negatively evaluated as bad, ugly, or boring. First we must solve the essential problem, particularly since this leads to the emergence of a certain onto-existential problem.

Without joining in the disputes between theorists, let us pass to the analysis of musical composition on the basis of direct experience. We shall take as examples such works indisputably belonging to music as Beethoven's Fifth Symphony or Chopin's B Flat Minor Sonata. They possess artistic or aesthetic value, but this aspect will remain outside the scope of our analysis. And I will not consider works that, although they are musical works, form an organic whole with a particular literary work, say Wagner's music dramas, other operas, and songs, irrespective of their type. The presence of a literary element makes the whole situation very complex, leading to the creation of a new artistic work that goes beyond pure music. In particular, the question of the identity and totality of a musico-literary work is quite different from that of a pure musical work; but I do not exclude from discussion so-called program music, which represents a special type of pure music, posing problems that should not be ignored.

Sounds, tones, and sound-constructs of a higher order and of varying types (as well as various whispers and knocks— as we have learned from modern music) constitute an essential element of every musical work. In employing the term "sound" and its cognates, I am not quite precise. "Sounds," in the sense of processes or objects persisting and taking place here and now in real time and constituting the elements of specific performances, do *not* belong to the musical work

itself. Both the reasons for my choice and the precise meaning of "sound" intended here in connection with the musical
work will become clear. Conversely, not every sound, tone,
or sound-construct—in this new sense and also in the sense
of individual processes or objects in the real world—forms
part of a work or, to put it more clearly, creates such a work,
even where there is a multiplicity of such constructs. For
example, sound-constructs that constitute the sound aspects
of linguistic constructs—acoustic signals, various sounds
occurring in nature, like the so-called songs of birds—do not
constitute musical works. What, then, are the differences
between a musical composition and such sound-constructs
or acoustic facts?

These differences might be manifest in three ways. They
might depend on (1) a specific ordering of sounds or sound-
constructs in their co-presence and succession; (2) the appearance in a musical work of quite new elements that
are different from sounds, sound-structures, whispers, and
knocks; (3) something quite specific that differentiates every
musical work, and even its individual phases, from the acoustic signals and auditory phenomena in nature.

Concerning (1): though at first there might often appear an
ordering of co-present and successive formations of sound
and sound-constructs different from the auditory phenomena of nature or acoustic signals, nevertheless that ordering
does not constitute the essential difference between musical
works and other auditory constructs. The order in a particular signal may be exactly like that of a given musical composition or part of it, and yet the two constructs will differ essentially. Thus, for example, the "Polish whistle," once used by
Polish students abroad as a recognition signal, constituted
three notes from the "Chimes" aria in Moniuszko's *Haunted
Manor,* but does not form part of the opera nor is it itself a
musical work. Had the sound order constituted the essential

difference between the constructs under discussion, then, conversely, its identical structure in both instances would have eliminated the difference between the two constructs. Thus, at the very least, it is not differences in the order of sound and sound-structures that are responsible for the constructs' separate identities.

With regard to (2): many theorists are inclined to think that certain new elements not present in other sound constructs emerge in a musical work and that it is precisely these elements that are characteristic of the work. But opinions diverge when we inquire what these new elements are and whether their presence is sufficient for the emergence of an essential difference between musical works and other acoustic structures.

Some point out that musical compositions include such constructs as melody, harmony, rhythm, and specific tempi. Moreover—as recent investigations show—a melody is not simply a sequence of sounds but something quite new in relation to them, namely, a certain gestalt quality[1] that only as its

1. See for example E. Kurth, *Musikpsychologie* (Berlin, 1931). However, the description given by S. Ossowski in his *U Podstaw Estetyki* (Warsaw, 1933) [*The Foundations of Aesthetics,* tr. J. W. Rodziński (Boston, 1978)] does not seem accurate. He writes that "melody is a sequence of intervals, expressed within the framework of rhythm" (p. 42), with "interval" being defined as "a relation of pitch" of sounds (p. 40). First of all, "sequence" is a certain relation, so a melody would then become a certain relation of relations. It may be that such a relation of relations must objectively exist between the sounds if melody is to exist and present itself to us in experience. But the relation of relations is not the melody itself, and it is the melody rather than this relationship that is perceived. The melody is the element of the musical work we hear, rather than the relation of relations between sounds that forms its objective conditioning. This type of relation of relations may only be an object of our intellectual definitions, whereas the melody, as a specific line of sounds developing in time and containing certain elements of movement and its related rhythm (or, if you

base has a number of variously pitched sounds but is not identical with them and is even to some extent independent of them. It seems that rhythm and the other above-mentioned elements of a musical work are also a gestalt quality. Whatever they may be, and although they distinguish many musical works from acoustic signals and auditory phenomena in nature, these features are not characteristic of musical works. It is debatable, for instance, whether every musical work must contain a melody. We could, in fact, take the whole of modern music as proof that there is no necessity for melody in a musical work. The same applies to the harmony absent from songs sung in unison. It may be, however, that rhythm, fixed in at least some sections, and—despite *tempo rubato*— a certain tempo character, determined at least for specific phases of the work, must appear in every musical work. But again we have to insist that precisely the same phenomena of melody, rhythm, tempo, and harmonic constructs appearing in certain musical works may also appear in acoustic signals and that these signals are not thereby transformed into musical works. Thus, the horn in Wilhelm II's limousine sounded a motif from Wagner's *Siegfried*. Thus, nowadays a number of radio stations use fragments of musical compositions as their signatures, but these applications are significant only as rec-

---

will, a certain kind of a sound stream, mobile and becoming and saturated with sound coloring), is what we directly hear as a qualitative whole where only an analysis is capable of discovering the individual sounds. Whoever moves away from the melody perceived in this manner to "a relation of pitch" abandons the realm of artistic products or aesthetic objects given us in experience and instead reflects upon the equivalence of certain mental operations that at best are in a certain way in conformity with aesthetic objects. This is a move from an organized, harmonized unity of the perceived whole to an atomized multiplicity of elements received only hypothetically but not appearing as palpable elements in a musical work.

ognition signals, not as music. Similarly, the appearance of characteristic rhythms in purely ritual and religious phenomena (drumming among African tribes) demonstrates that rhythm is not the element that distinguishes music from other acoustic phenomena. Some, it is true, might see in this last example a relationship between music and ritualistic religious phenomena, but such a relationship does not yet amount to an identity of kind. We may doubt whether so-called dance music, when employed only as a means of keeping the dancers in step and arousing in them a specific passion for expression through movement, is music in the strict sense of the word; that is, whether it is an artistic phenomenon, even when works that are undoubtedly music, such as Chopin's waltzes, are employed for the purpose. But this is already a problem in itself, as is the question of whether so-called artistic dances differ essentially as works of art from ritual dances or from the dance as a means of kinetic and rhythmic expression by people specifically excited by dance music. Just as artistic dance and such works as Chopin waltzes should be included among works of art, the dance as ritual phenomenon or human expression should be classified with extra-artistic phenomena, birdsongs, and the like, independently of their distinguishable elements of rhythm, melody, and tempo. This really is a matter of delimiting artistic phenomena and aesthetic objects, not of discovering the essential characteristics of musical compositions and the extent to which they are artistic.

According to other theories, an essential yet nonsounding element in a musical work is its "expression" of certain feelings or experiences or psychic facts, of its "representation" of this or that. There are, as we know, a number of distinguished musical works of a programmatic variety. Because of their expressiveness or representation, they are thought to incorporate something that is assumed to be a leading, if not an essential, function of music. Since the expression and what is expressed are supposed to constitute essential elements of a musical work, and expressiveness is identified with "representation," it is difficult to ascertain the limits of program music. As a result of this imprecise notion of expressiveness, it is not clear, according to this theory, whether only program music should be classified as music or whether it is only one type among many.

I shall return to this matter, but irrespective of how it is to be settled, it is crucial to our problem that neither expression nor representation is confined to music or even to art as such and that the same applies to that which is expressed or represented. On the contrary, expression and representation are by their nature and origin extra-musical and even extra-artistic phenomena, arising most often in the interpersonal relationships of everyday life, where neither what expresses nor what is expressed has anything to do with music or with art generally. Those who understand this function of expression or representation in others do not for a moment suppose, when they personally are deeply affected, for example, by a cry of despair that they are experiencing works of art or musical works in particular. Even assuming that, after clarifying the concept of expression or representation and what may be expressed or represented, we were to agree that something of this nature is present in every musical work, we would not thereby single out something differentiating, in a characteristic way, works of music from extra-musical works.

One hears sometimes the assertion that a musical work ought to evoke certain feelings in the listener or, more generally, bring about certain psychic states and that herein lies a work's specific essence. We know, however, that one and the same musical work may on different occasions, depending on performance and the circumstances of performance, evoke totally different feelings or even no feelings at all. It does not appear therefore that such evocation constitutes an essential or characteristic feature. Many objects and events which have nothing at all to do with music or art in general evoke a variety of feelings and other psychic states. Finally, where the evocation of feelings or psychic states occurs, if it occurs at all, it is but one of the ways in which the work affects the listener. Do we really have to conclude that a musical work possesses no essential structure or collection of characteristic properties that are purely its own—that what is characteristic must be sought in how the music affects the listener and not in the work itself?

Concerning (3): we have seen the failure of various attempts at pointing to some new, and in particular nonacoustic, element of a musical work, to differentiate it from acoustic signals and sound phenomena in nature. We must therefore consider what (if any) specific difference arises among the constructs under consideration. Before dealing with this I must point to a fact that may help us to move forward in our inquiry.

The view that at least some musical works perform the function of expressing or representing suggests that in this respect there is a real kinship between music and literature. Since the literary work can perform both these functions, because of the presence within its field of a stratum of linguistic sounds and associated meanings, it is suggested that music, too, has meanings whose bearers would, for example, be specific musical elements. Many theorists of music have spoken of the "meaning" which is supposedly encapsulated in specific musical works. Unfortunately, the meaning of "meaning" remains unclear and we often use the term in several different senses. Thus, we have the thesis in *La pensée musicale* by Combarieu, the distinguished historian of music, that so-called musical thoughts appear in musical works. The author's arguments are interesting and are backed by numerous examples from specific musical works. Yet the essential concept of "musical thought" is not satisfactorily explained, and, in this respect, the whole book fails. Combarieu probably does not mean by "meaning" the content of a linguistic inscription in any language. If the argument were that "meaning" in music is the same as the meaning of a sentence or any linguistic construct we would have to regard this view as false. A musical work (within the bounds under discussion) contains neither the sounds of words in any language nor meanings associated with these sounds nor the meanings of any sentences or clusters of sentences. This fact is perhaps trivial, but must be stated because it is important both for determining the specific structure of a musical work and for the question of its identity. A composition of (pure) music is not a literary work, and despite certain features that appear in both media (e.g., both have a quasi-temporal structure) the musical work is not, in its characteristic structure, similar to a literary work. Above all, as a direct result of the fact that no linguistic constructs and, in particular, no verbal and sentimental meanings are in a musical work, intentional states of affairs designated by the sense of the sentences and objects (things, people, events, and processes) presented through these states of affairs or designated by names appearing in literary works, cannot appear as elements of a musical composition. A musical work also has no place for aspects, be they schematized or concrete, that are actualized in a literary work by linguistic elements (specifically assigned that function) and that constitute one of the essential elements of a literary work of art. When listening to a musical work, if we often imagine certain objective situations, things and people in certain states, if we imaginatively actualize certain aspects of objects, then—assuming we are not dealing with complex musico-literary works like songs—we *eo ipso* step beyond the content of the musical work itself. At most, under a work's influence, we may succumb to fantasies of a literary nature that not only can but should drop away without doing harm to faithful perception of the given musical work, for they pollute this perception and make it difficult to attain in its pure form.

For a work of art to have a stratified structure, it is necessary and sufficient (a) that it should contain diverse elements —in a literary work, say, linguistic sounds, meanings, and presented objects; (b) that the homogeneous elements, that is, for example, linguistic auditory constructs, should combine into constructs of a higher order (as, for example, the meanings of words into meaningful sentences) and these in turn into constructs of a yet higher order (for instance, sentences combined into groups of sentences) until all constructs are linked into a single basic element permeating the whole work (i.e., the stratum of meaning in a literary work, though not that of aspects where various exceptions may occur); (c) that the basic element thus formed should not lose its distinctiveness and separateness within the totality of the work but should remain a distinguishable member and that this should happen both when we observe the work in its own structure and when we take it in the form in which it appears in aesthetic perception; and finally (d) that among the various basic elements of this type there should be an organic connection (that is, flowing from the essence of these elements) binding them into the totality of a single work. As I have shown elsewhere, a literary work consists of four strata, and a painting of at least two. But a work of pure music is not characterized by a stratified structure: it has only one stratum. Although a musical work is not homogeneous, nevertheless its diverse elements are not related into strata in the sense in question.

A stratified structure, which is proper to literature, is altogether alien to musical works. As a consequence, the latter lacks the polyphony of heterogeneous aesthetically valuable qualities and of the qualities of aesthetic values themselves. In a literary work this polyphony flows from the diversity of the material of its strata, a diversity absent in a musical work. But it does not follow from this that everything appearing in a musical work, an element, or just a dependent feature, should be homogeneous, or even that everything should be a sound or, in general, possess an acoustic character. On the contrary, despite what Hanslick seems to have said in his *On the Beautiful in Music,*[2] I will endeavor to show that it is the various nonsounding elements in musical compositions that play the chief role in musical "beauty." They do not form separate strata in the work, nor in particular do they constitute a distinct stratum in relation to what constitutes sound, or a certain structured cluster of sounds. They are so closely tied to sounds and sound-constructs that the musical work forms an extremely compact and cohesive whole and in this respect outshines work in the other arts, especially literature. When Nicolai Hartmann in his book *Das Problem des geistigen Seins* borrows my concept of the stratified character of a literary work and applies it somewhat mechanically to the remaining art forms, including music, he alters radically the concept I have introduced, of "stratum" in a work of art, and he conflates this, and its presence for the observer, with the function of representation that is performed by one of the work's elements in relation to another, the latter therefore having its ontic base in the former. One should not uncritically apply structures revealed in works of one art to those of another art. Let us clarify this matter further.

2. I have the impression that Hanslick is often credited with statements he himself would regard as too radical. A fresh analysis of his views is due.

After analyzing the literary work, when I turned in 1928 to analysis of the other arts, I was unpleasantly surprised to find that stratification is absent from musical works. Before I realized that the concept of stratified structure cannot be applied to music, I had expected that it would be possible to define all works of art in terms of this structure and that it would be relatively easy to pinpoint their difference from all other objects. Musical works broke away from what I had considered a universal rule. I had to find some other way to distinguish works of art from other objects, especially from objects constituting the products of creative acts of consciousness. This made the task considerably more difficult. If, therefore, despite the theoretical inconvenience, I rejected the notion of a stratified musical work, it was only because of very powerful arguments. As I have observed, Hartmann confuses the notion of a stratum in a work of art, as I have just described it, with a quite different concept of stratum that he does not clearly define. He takes the new concept merely as a guideline in understanding works of art and other cultural products. I think that his notion could be defined thus: objects of a certain kind in relation to objects of another kind constitute a stratum (in this new sense) when (1) the former constitute an ontic base for the latter, and they achieve this function because (2) the former intentionally designate the latter. This second function may take various forms. Thus, in a stable linguistic system, the sound of a word designates its meaning and enables us to select, out of all possible meanings, the one with which the sound is connected. The meaning of a name or of a sentence generates intentionally and designates the corresponding presented object (or thing or state of affairs), an aspect reveals a certain object, and so on.

If the new concept of stratum is defined thus, it cuts across my own concept of substratum as defined above and employed in my book *The Literary Work of Art*. That which performs the function of an ontic base and intentionally designates something else does not have to be a stratum of a work of art (in my sense) and need not be its constituent at all. For example, a performance of a musical work, which is not in any sense a constitutive element of the work, does fulfill the functions of an ontic base and intentional designation, even though the performance is not the work's only ontic base. Similarly, pigments constitute the ontic base of a painting and designate it intentionally, but they do not constitute an element of the painting and do not form any of its strata, in my sense, although they would in Hartmann's sense, were it desirable to use this sense at all. Similarly, the concrete voice material constitutes the (partial) ontic base and designates the sound of words constituting the literary work, yet the material itself remains outside the work. Finally, in relation to a melody, specific sounds perform the two functions of a stratum in Hartmann's sense and yet do not constitute a stratum of a musical work in my sense, even though they form one of its elements. There are, nevertheless, elements of a work of art, say the aspects of a picture, that constitute a stratum of the work in both the senses I have distinguished.

In view of overlap in the scope of these two concepts, it will be best not to apply the same term to both. I will retain "stratum" to designate my concept. I favor this distinction because the stratum in my sense may, in relation to certain elements in the work, perform functions that are characteristic of "stratum" in Hartmann's sense, and yet not be a stratum in the first sense in relation to these elements. Thus, the "stratum" of objects presented in a literary work sometimes performs in some of its aspects the function of revealing what I have called metaphysical qualities and constitutes for them the ontic base. Yet it is not distinguished, in relation to these qualities, as a separate "stratum." On the contrary, these qualities are strictly connected with the presented objects.

The fact that Hartmann did not distinguish these two concepts of "stratum" (*Schicht*) has led him to ascribe to a literary work a considerably greater number of strata than it has. It has undoubtedly persuaded him also to regard a musical work as a stratified construct and to include as part of the work the elements of its performance, and this is, strictly speaking, nonsense.

If, however, a musical work has only one stratum, and if neither a particular order of co-present and successive sounds and sound-constructs of a higher order (nor various nonsounding elements) are sufficient to distinguish a musical composition either from acoustic signals or sounding phenomena in nature, at first sight it seems that we lose all justification for carrying out the distinction under discussion. The distinction between, say, Beethoven's *Pathétique Sonata,* or any other musical work, and all signals and sounding phenomena in nature is so compelling that it is difficult to doubt it, even though this difference does not emerge clearly until we assume an aesthetic attitude and apprehend a musical work as a specific aesthetic object. The actual aesthetic value, if any, of what is presented to us is not relevant, since we experience an aesthetic object not only when we recognize its great value but also when we realize that it is ugly, boring, or banal. We do not, when we feel like it, assume an attitude in which aesthetic experience evolves; voluntarily but only when works of art, including music heard in a particular performance, have the ability to evoke this attitude or mood, whether or not they are successful. We must therefore inter alia analyze the musical work to find the cause of this effect, which therefore might distinguish the work from other sounding phenomena. Both sounding phenomena in nature and acoustic warning signs are particular real events or processes in the real world. While this is beyond doubt for natural sounding phenomena like the singing of birds, an acoustic sound, like a car horn, is also a real fact and must be so understood by pedestrians if it is to act as a warning signal. At the same time, the very occurrence of the signal points to the actual occurrence of another real fact.[3]

By contrast, a musical work, given as an aesthetic object on the basis of a particular performance, is not a real event lasting during the performance and for that reason cannot designate any other objects or processes occurring in the real world. The same is true of the performance as a whole.[4] While writing, for instance, if I once again hear through the wall that Chopin prelude, I realize incidentally, without interrupting my work, that my neighbor is again practicing or that she has just returned home. The fact of the musical work's performance leads me to another real fact: my neighbor's practicing or her return home. But recognition of this fact is not necessary. I may concentrate exclusively on the performance itself, noticing its shortcomings and excellencies; the heard performance of the musical work does not then have the function of a sign or signal. Furthermore, captivated by a particularly good performance of the prelude, I begin to listen attentively; steeped in this listening I soon forget my neighbor or her return and commune directly with the prelude itself, listening carefully to its details. Then

---

3. It was Husserl who had already pointed out in his *Logical Investigations* (volume 2, part 1, section 1, "An ambiguity in the term 'sign'") that what he called "signs" (*Zeichen*) and "designations" (*Anzeichen*) are, unlike linguistic expressions, real constructs designating real constructs and facts.

4. Many musicologists argue that a musical composition indicates in some way the composer's experiences and his mental qualities, and even various circumstances of his life. I shall take this up presently.

apparently even the performance disappears from my experience, while the prelude itself, as an object of aesthetic experience, lacks the character of an event just then occurring or of some other real object in the world. Directed toward this aesthetic experience, I seem to forget about my real surroundings and commune with something complete in itself. If it is a pure musical composition and not one linked with a literary work (a poem, say), then its content does not connect with real processes or events in the world.[5] Even where certain works or their parts have the function of expressing mental states or of representing objects (*Darstellung* rather than *Vorstellung*), as in Debussy's *Nuages,* then what is expressed or represented is not object or experience occurring in the real world but a fictitious construct.

But, the reader might ask, is not a musical work a cultural product woven into the complete tapestry of the life of a particular individual and of the social, economic, political, and cultural relations of a given historical period? Is it not stamped with the spirit of the times? Since it came into being at a particular moment in time, does it not ipso facto belong to our real world?

It is undoubtedly true that musical works are produced by real individuals who do not form a system isolated from the real human and nonhuman world. They are surely connected in many ways with the surrounding organic and living world, especially with the world of contemporary human beings, and this fact influences the works that are produced. It is at least probable that from a work's properties we could infer the character of its creator and the creator's surrounding world. But we must guard against drawing conclusions sole-

5. Regarding the content of a musical work and its intentional structure, cf. chapter 5 below, and also *The Literary Work of Art,* section 20, and *Does the World Exist?,* volume 2, section 45.

ly derived from speculations regarding, say, the author's love life and the extent to which the author's creative states have been conditioned by sexual processes; nor is it sufficient to examine only the social and economic conditions in which the work was formed. If anyone is interested in these kinds of dependencies and relationships between properties of works of art and of music especially, let him study them by all means, as long as he takes everything into account without distorting the picture of the world. But all these dependencies still do not prove that the product arising under real conditions, brought about by the author's real activity, must itself be something real and that its whole significance should be confined to such dependencies.

The fact that a musical work is a cultural product does not settle the question of its ontic status, for of course the question is wider than this and not confined to musical works. It includes all cultural products and not necessarily just artistic ones: here belong products of social life—those of the economy (e.g., currency), political life (e.g., state institutions), those of intellectual life (all products of scientific investigations). With regard to all these, we have to consider in what way they exist, if they exist at all, and it is doubtful whether these works of art exist in the same way as mountains, rivers, plants, animals, and human beings, if only because no physicist, chemist, geographer, or biologist has so far discovered within his scientific experience those types of objects to which all cultural products belong. This is the case also because the occurrence of cultural products requires special conditions that go beyond chemico-physical and biological facts. Even within the sphere of the psychosomatic existence of a human being, special behavior patterns are needed before there can be processes issuing in works of art or other cultural products. Moreover, in order to decide what causal and (if I may imperfectly but perhaps instruc-

tively say) thematic connections there are between works
of art and real facts in the world surrounding the artist (re-
membering that this is not only a world of purely physical, chemical, biological, and mental processes and events,
but also that strangely specific world of man, the world
of his culture), we have to perform two different cognitive
operations.

We have first to cognize the given cultural product, in this
instance the piece of music, with its own characteristics,
without importing anything extraneous, and second, to
cognize independently of these results those real and cultural
conditions under which the product has been formed. Only
when we have performed these two cognitive tasks and
compared the results independently obtained can we go on
to the further cognitive task of collating the results of the
two investigations. We may then consider what causal or
relational connections and what similarity or kinship occur
between them. Unfortunately, this task is often overlooked,
and there is no attempt at proper investigation of the properties of the cultural product itself. Even when this task is performed it is usually done imperfectly: the work is interpreted
a priori as a product of specific but not yet fully revealed
causal and cultural conditions, and various properties not
belonging to it are forced upon it. What is more, having carried through a forced interpretation without obtaining satis-
factory cognition of the work of art (or of some other cultural
product), we begin on the basis of the apparently cognized
work to put forward various hypotheses regarding the causal
and cultural conditions of its formation. Next, a new series of
fictitious attributes is forced upon the epoch in question.
That is, on the basis of a work's assumed properties, a "picture" is formulated of the epoch that, according to the general
hypothesis, contributed to the formation and the properties
of the work, and, conversely, a "picture" of the work is con-

structed on the basis of the allegedly cognized epoch of its origin. This procedure inevitably results in moving in a circle through a world it has largely conjured up.

The problem is not simple, either epistemologically or methodologically. The epoch in which a particular work was produced, say Chopin's lifetime, now belongs to the past. In our contemporary world we do not come across facts that we assume have contributed to the formation and the properties of the B Minor Sonata. If there is anything that we can know about this epoch and about the composer who was alive in it, this can only be indirect knowledge. If we ourselves had witnessed certain facts, we could refer only to our memories or the memories of others; but once those have died who were contemporary with Chopin and the creation of his works, the conditions under which the B Minor Sonata was created can be inferred only from legacies and relics. We have the various physical relics (say, Napoleon's pipe, Mickiewicz's quill pen, Chopin's manuscripts, as well as houses they inhabited and the instruments on which they played—e.g., Chopin's piano, if it still exists) that they had either created themselves or at least had used. But if we confine ourselves to examining the physical qualities of objects, such as the manuscripts, if we do not agree that the essential qualities embodied in them also include certain, as we call them, "spiritual" products—that is, specifically, if we do not agree that Chopin has left compositions from which we can indirectly decipher a world long ago vanished and in which Chopin composed—then, apart from secondary detail,[6] we shall not be able to recreate the cultural situation of those times.

In other words, we must start from communion with the

---

6. Some of these details may have a certain significance: for instance, the fact that the pianos on which Chopin performed were considerably different from present-day instruments.

cultural product itself (say, the B Minor Sonata), which still somehow exists today, which we somehow reach in our aesthetic experience, even though various details of performance and the conditions of listening considerably obstruct and often falsify our conclusions. Only as a result of cognizing that work will we be able to infer the conditions of its composition, including its dependence on or independence of these conditions. Naturally, we shall be in a position in which we will have to make use of other indirect information about the past, but we must proceed so that these sources of information (other cultural products or relics of the past) become cognitively accessible to us, irrespective of the outcome of our coming to know the cultural product from which we deduce the circumstances of its composition. Otherwise, we are faced with the inevitable *circulus in probando*.

We can never achieve more than the mutual confrontation, support, and control of information about the past derived indirectly from works that have come down to us from that epoch. We cannot directly reach that epoch once it is past. In fact, we employ works to comment upon other works, rather than using past reality to comment upon them. Hence, the possibility of our cognizing the contents of works that are directly accessible to us now is the condition of our being able to come to know the past, and not vice versa, as art historians often assume. If by this indirect method we wish to conclude something about past creative processes, say Chopin's when composing his *Revolutionary Etude,* we must make yet another very basic but not obvious assumption that a composition Chopin produced is exactly identical with the work we hear today.

I cannot enter in detail into this complicated epistemological and methodological question, although it is fundamental for the methodology of the humanities. But assuming that we must first in any event interrogate the musical work itself about its properties, let us inquire whether, as a result of what we find in it, we can say that it is a real process, event, or object.

Every real object, process, or event has a specific spatio-temporal location or duration. Whenever I confront a real object, it is here and now, where I am present. A performance of the B Minor Sonata is undoubtedly occurring here and now, either when I play it or when I listen to a performance of it, but we cannot say this of the sonata itself. This is so, irrespective of the fact that the "now" varies and may apply equally to the performance by Chopin himself when he played the work publicly for the first time. Did the sonata exist then, and was it in the room where Chopin played it? Where? Is it in the room, in the piano, is it above the piano, under it, or beside it? And when it is played simultaneously in ten different places, as may have occurred many times, is this one and the same sonata simultaneously in ten various places? This is obvious nonsense. In the sonata's contents, in its specific chords and melodies and harmonies, there are no features or elements that in any way establish its specific location in real space or constitute that location. There are no such features, and the work's whole structure shows that this would not be possible. And this is why the very question "Where is the B Minor Sonata?" sounds so absurd.

Before considering the analogous problem of placing the B Minor Sonata or any other musical work in time, I want to consider another question connected with the possible reality of a musical work. Neither the musical work as a whole nor any of its specific parts is "individual" or "particular" in the way that every real object is, say, the paper on which a particular edition of the score of Beethoven's Fifth Symphony has been printed. When we listen to a specific performance in a purely aesthetic attitude, we seem to gather from the specific sounds or higher-order sound-constructs

pure qualities and qualitative musical clusters that are not
individualized on account of their real existence. Listening to
a specific performance with our attention on the work itself,
we seem involuntarily to ignore the individual mode of existence of the currently occurring individual concrete sounds.
We extract from the manifest *concretum* the composition itself, constructed from nonindividualized qualities, namely,
the individual B Minor Sonata itself. How this comes about,
why we succeed in this process, and why we do it, although
not deliberately or very consciously (though not uncon-
sciously), are further questions with which I cannot deal here.
The essential issue here is whether I am right in thinking that
what we are concerned with in the perception of a musical
work itself is not in this sense a particular in the way that
material objects or perceptions of them are.

And this contention will doubtless evoke objections from
many readers. Can it be true, they may say, that the B Minor
Sonata is not a particular? Is it not, on the contrary, something so specific that its duplication is not possible and that
therefore it is supremely a particular?

Undoubtedly this sonata, like every work of art which is
truly valuable and unlike any hack work, adaptation, or im-
itation, is certainly an individual in a special sense. But we
must try to see in what sense this is true. The particularity of
a genuine work of art differs from the particularity of a real
object or a concrete mental process. Its particularity is not
tied to a unique position in real time and space and does not
stem from a mode of existence such as is proper to all real
objects in the strict sense of the word. The B Minor Sonata is
not individuated via a *particularization* characteristic of real
modes of existence, but via a specific, unrepeatable selection. Harmonization of qualities appears in such a context of
auditory or other qualities that it experiences a certain specific, qualitative modification that it would not have under-

gone, were the selection of qualities even slightly different. In this modification the quality simultaneously modifies its surroundings, which would not have been what they are had the qualitative modification undergone change in relation to the shape that the quality has precisely in that uniquely co-alesced consonance of qualities.[7] The outcome of this conso-nance and mutual modification is a certain ultimate quality of the whole that either manifests itself in the specific phases of the work or constitutes itself definitely in the successive phases as the dominant quality of the whole work—emanat-ing from the dynamics of the phases. This quality is so spe-cific that it has not and cannot have a duplicate unless that other work is its perfect replica in a concrete performance during which, in fact, that final quality has manifested itself. It is that dominant, ultimate quality that determines the par-ticularity of a musical work, and, it is worth stressing, this quality need not be purely a quality of sound, for, as we shall see, various elements may constitute its qualitative basis and determine its ultimate definition. With the exception of con-scious experiences, there is perhaps no other field in which Bergson's thesis about the motley qualitative continuum

7. Where the musical work is complete and fully notated, the thesis regarding the mutual modification of the qualities of particular sounds and of the dominant, auditory wholes can be tested experimentally. Since the score is available, we can establish which elementary parts lie at the base of the synthetic consonances of qualities because we can, reading the score independently, produce specific sounds and specific sound-constructs of a higher order and then link them together. We can thus demonstrate to ourselves, purely experimentally, that they do modify one another, and how, against their background and on the basis of their mutual adjust-ment, there arises a dominant gestalt of a certain phase, and then of the multiphased whole of the work. One must, of course, be capable of hear-ing this and of discovering the ties between the elements and the phases of the work.

vindicates itself as convincingly as in music. It is here too, perhaps, that it is possible most decisively to arrive at a clear grasp of gestalt qualities, which are the subject of gestalt psychology, except that here we are not concerned with mental facts but with products given us as objects of experience. With this reservation we may accept the several experimental analyses of actual musical works carried out by Ernst Kurt in his *Musikpsychologie* (Berlin, 1931) as completely accurate.

This purely qualitative particularity, as I shall call it, of a musical work (which, incidentally, also characterizes works of other types, especially lyrics and architecture), differs fundamentally from the particularity of real objects. This particularity stems from their mode of existence, from the individuating concretion of ideal qualities in various real objects. This individuation is, in turn, strictly connected with a univocal temporal determination and, where possible—that is, in the case of all extended objects—also with a univocal determination of spatial location. The purely qualitative particularity is characteristic of the musical composition itself, so long as it is a genuine work of art, while only specific performances are subject to that second kind of individuation. Whoever is able, on the basis of hearing a certain concrete performance, to attain in aesthetic perception the musical work itself also attains its qualitative particularity and realizes its supraparticular character vis-à-vis the spatio-temporal particularity of real objects.

A musical work is, however, not only "supraparticular" but, in a sense that I shall presently attempt to define, also "supratemporal," in contrast to its specific performances that are univocally fixed in time. In the investigations of musical compositions a more precise clarification is required of the various concepts of "temporality," "supratemporality," and "atemporality," which are usually jumbled together.

Consequently, the investigation of the musical composition itself yields different results.

If we consider the musical work as being, from a certain point in time, a finished product of the composer's creative activity, a product that in all its parts exists from the moment when it came into being as a whole (when at the same time we comprehend it "at one go" as a whole designated by the score), then we have to agree that, say, Chopin's B Minor Sonata is an object which endures in time. What enables it to persist in time and whether this duration is precisely like that of certain real objects are matters to be investigated. At this moment the only significant fact about this object is that, in contrast with quite differently constituted objects, namely, processes and events, it has a structure like that of objects persisting in time. The fact that it came into being at a particular moment in time also rules out the notion that a musical work is an ideal object like, say, a number.

If, however, we consider a musical work with regard only to its content presented to us in a direct aesthetic cognition as we listen to one of its performances, then all its various phase-parts are revealed gradually, and the question of the work's temporality or supratemporality appears in a different manner. This happens when we succeed in concentrating on the work itself, distinguishing it from particular performances and generally from the processes and events occurring in the real world during its performance. The musical work will then reveal itself to us as a supratemporal object in a special sense and characterized at the same time by an internal, immanent, quasi-temporal structure.[8]

More precisely, every real process in the real world takes

---

8. It may seem puzzling that a twofold investigation of a musical composition is at all possible. I attempt to demonstrate this in *Does the World Exist?*, volume 1, sections 26–28, and volume 2, section 59.

place at a specific, determined time that is not and cannot be repeated. The process spans a certain period, although by itself it never constitutes a full saturation of that period. Full saturation is constituted by all the processes taking place over that period throughout the universe. Whenever such a process appears in our external or internal perception, it carries upon itself and upon all its phases a specific stamp of temporal determination. That stamp penetrates it completely and derives from the qualitative determination of the phases or moments it saturates. Naturally, this qualitative determination of temporal moments and phases characterizes only the phases and moments of concretely experienced time,[9] not of so-called objective time, or astronomical time measured with appropriate instruments. Objective, measurable, astronomical time does not enter into the characterization of concretely given processes and events. The question arises of how we are to characterize the temporality of a particular performance of a musical work to which we must listen in its entirety if it is to be given to us *in concreto* as a musical work in all its phase-parts. Well, the qualitative determination, or, we might say, the coloring of the temporal phase, depends on a complete range of processes and events that occur in that phase and are accessible to the subject of consciousness in direct experience. The coloring is also dependent in a particular synthetic way on the temporal coloring of the preceding moment not yet extinguished in the experiencing of the present. If, therefore, a certain individual sound or sound-construct of a higher order, which forms

9. In this outline of a concretely experienced time, on the whole I follow Bergson's well-known analysis of concrete duration and the more profound treatment of this subject by Husserl in his *Phenomenology of Inner Time-Consciousness*. My own further investigations will be found in *The Literary Work of Art* and in chapter 2 of *The Cognition of the Literary Work*.

part of a certain performance of a musical work, occurs at time t within the perceptual range of a certain psychological subject, then the concrete coloring of that moment is co-determined by the appearance at that moment of that sound or sound-construct and whatever else fills that moment. This concrete, temporal coloring appears to envelop the sound structure. If a particular, concrete sound-construct takes up a lengthy period of time, then the specific phases filling the given phases of that period of time are characterized by the appropriate temporal coloring. They influence each other synthetically, in that a later sound-phase of that sound structure depends for its temporal coloring on the coloring of the earlier phases. It is these temporal colorings, together with the synthetically consonant qualities of the concrete sound structure, that co-define the particularity of a concrete sound structure and make it, in the fullness of its qualities, unrepeatable. When we perform the same work again, the concrete, temporal coloring of the specific phases of this new performance are quite different from the temporal coloring of the phases of the previous performance. The coloring is so new that it rules out an identity between the two performances, despite the possibility of a great similarity between them.

The temporal stamp is closely connected with the concrete sound-construct, although in itself it is not, of course, a sound or an audible phenomenon at all. If, for instance, at a certain concert we are concentrating on the ongoing performance of a musical work because, say, we happen to be interested in the way the artist is playing (rather than in what he is playing), we then perceive the work not only as something taking place in the real world here and now but also in its qualitative determination as a whole and, hence, in its temporal coloring. We cannot separate the one from the other: a particular (and of its kind, unique) continuum of

changes in the qualitative temporal coloring is interwoven
with the phases of the performance. To put it in a better way,
it is the qualitatively determined kind of such colorings that
is absent. What they have in common is only the structure of
changes and temporal perspectives, that structure responsible for the fact that, despite the unrepeatability of the qualitative temporal coloring, one unique time constitutes itself
in direct experience: it flows irreversibly in one direction.
Every performance of a musical work occurs in a different
temporal span, for each has a different temporal coloring,
or rather, a different, developing continuum of temporal
colorings.

By contrast, the musical composition, as such, totally
lacks all those temporal colorings that characterize its performances. The composer could not have foreseen the temporal colorings of the time spans during which his work
would be performed, since he does not have at his disposal
any means of designating the future temporal colorings in
the score and cannot endow a work with mutually exclusive
determinations. Nor does the work carry those temporal
colorings that have acquired for the composer a concrete
shape in the course of his own first effective performance, if
any, of the work. There is after all no technical way of mark-
ing these temporal colorings in the score.[10]

As we learn from the preceding argument, the concrete
temporal coloring of particular performances of the same
work stems only partly from the qualitative determination

10. Naturally, the matter would be different if such a first performance
were to be preserved on a good gramophone record. Still, this would just
be the recording of the first performance and would not constitute the
work itself, if only because that particular performance could have been
imperfect. The fact that the composer himself was the performer would
not guarantee the performance's perfection.

of the work itself. To a large extent these colorings are, on each occasion, co-determined by the circumstances in which a given performance occurs: circumstances that, as far as the work is concerned, are individual and differ for each occasion. Nor would there be any point in the composer endowing his work with the temporal coloring characteristic of a certain performance, for it would not be possible ever again to perform the work exactly in that manner. In fact, a musical work, unlike painting and architecture and like literature, the theatre, and film, is by its nature designed so that there should be many performances of it and the various performances should strike the listener as being of one and the same work. For the listener who perceives a performance of a musical work in an aesthetic attitude and attempts to reach the work itself, it is natural to some degree to try to ignore or dampen those modifications of the temporal colorings that flow from the given performance—just as he does in the case of minor departures from the score during a performance. In doing this, the listener appears to be reaching after the work in its own endowment, shelling from it the *concretum* of a given performance. If he succeeds in this, the work appears as an object of aesthetic perception without those secondary temporal colorings arising from the particular performance, and the work is in that sense supratemporal. It is only the apprehension of a musical work in this supratemporality that makes possible the discovery of its own unique temporal structure.[11] As we inquire into this structure, the

11. How and to what extent we succeed in hearing the work itself, in its own endowment and without the modification of temporal coloring arising from the circumstances of a given performance, is one of the central problems in the inquiry into the perception of a musical work and the conditions of the objectivity of such perception.

supratemporality of the musical work will emerge more clearly.

Every musical work contains a number of phases or parts that normally succeed each other continuously, each of them either lasting a certain time or at least filling a unit of time. The order in which they are to appear is univocally determined in the score. Because of this order, a musical work, considered from beginning to end—that is, as its content appears to us when we perceive it aesthetically—possesses a special, seemingly temporal span, which changes into a strictly temporal one during performance. But it is only in performance that the musical work appears to become embodied. It is thus multiphased, like a literary work. Each real process is also multiphased, and although the musical work itself cannot be regarded as such a real process—for at the moment of its creation all its phases exist simultaneously, and it is only in performance that the work acquires this multiphased character—nevertheless it is, as such, envisaged as something which, in the course of a certain process, reveals its multiphased character. We might acknowledge this difference by saying that the musical work itself is quasi-temporal.

But we must be clear about the details of this quasi-temporal structure. Obviously we are not concerned with physical time apprehended mathematically and equated with the one-dimensional homogeneous continuum, but with concrete, phenomenal, qualitative time in which specific phases or moments are qualitatively determined in relation to what saturates those moments and in relation to the place of the given moments between other moments. The temporal structure of a musical work constitutes a special form of this kind of time. The work's particular phases appear in a temporal coloring designated exclusively by the musical structure of the given work in a given phase. Chopin's C Minor Prelude, Op. 25, No. 20, opens with the following chords:

The very first chord is distinguished by the fact that its pure sound elements do not exhaust the attributes of that first chord but include the special character of what appears in the initial phase of the work, which is to be preceded by no other element of the work. The chord also is used to signal that something is to follow. Designating it as "the beginning" gives it a certain temporal characterization in a purely formal sense that need not even have a temporal mode. Every mathematical sequence of numbers (say, that of the natural series) has a beginning in the sense of having a first number, which others follow, but there is no question of a temporal order. Similarly, in a musical work the strictly temporal character of its "beginning" will appear only in performance. In the work itself, it is rather a formal schema that becomes materially determined only by the fact that in a given work it is just such a cluster of sounds that happens to constitute the beginning. It is not the beginning of just any work, but specifically of the C Minor Prelude that opens

with such a cluster of sounds followed by another determined cluster.

Thus, the qualitative coloring of the beginning of this prelude does not, strictly speaking, depend solely on the filling-
out of the work's "first" moment, but also on the filling-out
of the immediately succeeding moments. Every change in
this filling-out would cause a change in the temporal coloring. Thus, had the first cluster of sounds been followed by
another cluster, which does not appear in the C Minor Prelude, the beginning itself would also acquire a slightly different coloring, for its dependent qualities are influenced by
what is to follow. We have thus a backward reflex, a modification of the preceding phase in the light of the one that
succeeds. Whoever hears the work for the first time is not
aware of this at the moment the work starts, and so the temporal coloring of the work's beginning does not constitute
itself fully for him: for the time being it is as though nothing
were to follow. But as soon as the next phase is sounded (the
preceding phase fading into the past), then that first phase,
together with its original temporal coloring, acquires the
character of an introduction to the second phase, that is, of
something from which the second phase emerges. The second phase completes the determination of the first phase as
its continuation and also modifies and completes the first
phase's temporal coloring. The second cluster of sounds is
followed by a third, which in turn acts as a continuation of
the second. Once again, therefore, the third phase reflects
upon the initial phase and the second phase that has just
passed.

When we listen to a second performance, having then at
least a sketchy acquaintance with the whole work, the first
cluster of sounds already announces the next one. It not only
is but also presents itself as something passing into the next
cluster of sounds. In a melody played *legato,* the first tone

imperceptibly changes into the succeeding phase. The tone stretching into the next phase must therefore be heard in this capacity at the outset. So it is only when we know the C Minor Prelude that the temporal coloring of its beginning reveals itself.

The stretch of this anticipation and regressive coloring of phases depends on the sound content of particular phases and on the way the work is constructed. Detailed studies of specific works would be necessary before we could be sure what different types are possible in this respect and on what the specific connection of the particular phases depends. But the fact that something like this does occur is indisputable, as is the fact that when one phase of a work anticipates the next, and the next phase does appear, then it fulfills the expectation, becomes the realization of what was anticipated, and thus becomes more closely connected with the preceding phase. What is more, the qualitative determination of the sounds forming part of this new phase undergoes a relative modification because it is preceded by that specific cluster of sounds. In this way, each phase except the initial one is co-defined, both in its relative aspects and in its temporal coloring, by the phases and temporal coloring of neighboring phases and also to some extent (depending on the work) by those that are more remote. The deeper this mutual co-determination, the wider its base in the neighboring phases: the more cohesive the structure of the work or its particular section. A musical unit of a higher order is thus constituted, both because of the connections between the clusters of sounds and because of the specific, temporal structure, which distinguishes this unit from all other musical structures as a self-contained, dependent unit. If, however, the specific parts of the work are more loosely knit, if they do not add up to a set of mutually dependent parts of a single, dominant sound-construct (a construct that forms a distinct element of that work), but merely succeed each other loosely, then the depth of the modifications of the temporal coloring of succeeding phases becomes superficial, the work drawn out, and perhaps even falling into ever new successive clusters of sounds whose progression lacks justification.

The fact that the connection may be very close between the sound clusters that succeed each other and may embrace a series of succeeding phases means that the "beginning" of a musical work need not be confined to the "opening" arrangement of sounds (to what in the C Minor Prelude constitutes the opening of the first bar; *see* p. 71) but may also include the whole first motif or theme and even the first musical phrase, that is, constructs already including a succession of phases or spread over a succession of phases. In all such "beginnings" in the extended sense of the word, we must, in considering the quasi-temporal coloring, distinguish the "beginning" in the narrow sense of the word (including of course its temporal coloring), namely, the initial sound cluster of the given work. This initial cluster is also the first member of a system of "moments" of the work, comprising the members of the whole temporal or quasi-temporal structure of a musical work—a structure unique to every composition. In strictly formal terms, these members succeed one another in a definite sequence according to the relationship of "before" and "after," but in this relationship they are at the same time qualitatively determined by the above-mentioned temporal coloring. They have their source in the filling-out with sounds of a given moment within the realm of the work itself. They may, on the one hand, constitute the preparation of the next phase or phases or, on the other, a continuation of the sound-constructs developed in the work's earlier phases. Neither is necessary for each phase of the work, because the work may include moments whose filling-out constitutes the apparent completion of a particular complex sound, stretching over a number of moments, without constituting the opening of the succeeding sound-constructs. It therefore does not pre-figure the work's succeeding phases. Conversely, there may be phases—moments that initiate a complex sound-construct but do not also form the closure of the preceding one. This type of phenomenon within the work's temporal structure entails the emergence of whole periods (or totalities of a higher order) of which the work as a whole consists. But the "moments" that may be distinguished within each of these periods are not—as someone transposing the structure of the continuum of real time on to a musical composition might suppose—temporal cross-sections constituting the sharp boundary of a precisely conceived present between a past and a future. The "moments" appearing in a musical work always have a certain temporal extension in relation to physical time in which the performance occurs; they are temporal concretes in contrast to the mentally, abstractly designated "cross-sections" of the continuum of homogeneous time. What is more, this extension is not the same for all moments of the musical work. It depends on the richness and structure of its sound saturation and of the musical forms that constitute themselves on this sound base. These forms decide what is to belong to that musical moment and what goes beyond its boundaries, assuming that we may speak of boundaries at all.

The "moments" in a musical work are certain temporal units determined by the sound base, units which distinguish themselves in the stream of the quasi-time of a work as something distinct from other units, although the transition from one to the other may be in various ways fluid and blurred and the boundary not sharp in every case. There are two reasons: the temporal structure of a work is not continuous in the sense of being a homogeneous continuum (1) because it is an arrangement of distinct members (moments) and (2) because the particular members, apart from a purely formal ordering into "before" and "after," are endowed with specific temporal coloring. So the "time" of a musical composition is not homogeneous; it is structurally and qualitatively organized, and the type and character of that organization depends on what sound structures fill out a particular moment or longer periods of the work as a whole. The distinction in this organization (in, say, two different compositions or in two different movements of the same composition) may also be marked in the qualitative differences of specific dynamics and tempo—the speed of time itself.

Since, however, the organization of musical time is, among other things, connected with the phenomenon of later phases being foreshadowed by the earlier ones, we have to make sure that such foreshadowing does in fact occur in at least some phases of the musical work. We here have the support of both positive and negative facts. In the course of the statement of a particular theme, its earlier phases announce phases yet to come, with greater or lesser precision, so that while the listener perceives the current phase and does not yet effectively hear the succeeding phases, he seems to experience the general direction in which the theme will turn. The forthcoming phase of the theme seems to sound in the listener's imagination and with its special shape determines the outline of the currently developing theme which is to enter into just this mobile shape of the theme's succeeding phase. If the listener's expectation proves correct, the succeeding phase of the theme when it is actually heard fulfills that expectation and enables the listener to engross himself in the thematic motion which has begun. But this does not always happen, the expectation is not always fulfilled, and this causes a feeling of surprise. A quite unexpected sound formation is heard, and musicians often speak of an "unexpected," yet artistically fully intended, resolution of the musical tension. It is perhaps precisely

these cases of unexpected resolutions, wherein the perspectives just opening up are abandoned, that offer the clearest
proof that in a musical work the earlier phases do in fact
foreshadow the later ones and that a perspective opens onto
the latter moments of the time immanent in the work. Irrespective of possible variants of this phenomenon, each phase
except the last of a musical work contains a "future" with
respect to further phases of the work that, by being anticipated, colors in a specific way the phase being actualized.
Sometimes the work's finale is also anticipated in this way,
without of course opening up perspectives onto any further
phases.[12] Only works characterized by quasi-temporal extension, that is, musical, literary, theatrical, and film compositions, can have such endings. The continuum of experienced real time does not have this type of ending. Even when
real objects determined in their temporality come to the end
of their existence, in the closing phase of their existence a
perspective always opens further temporal phases in which
other processes will take place and other objects persist in
time; but no such "afterward" is possible once the musical
work has come to an end. That is, the "afterward" is not
designated by the work itself, even in the most formal way. In
the same manner its content does not designate any "before"
that somehow stretches back to before the beginning of the
work. The organized quasi-time of the composition is complete at both ends and does not enter into the time-continuum
of the real world. For this reason a musical work's content is
not extended over any period of the history of the real world,
despite the fact that its content is distinguished by a structure

12. In modern music the finale is very often unexpected. The work
stops abruptly and it is only ex post facto that this is seen as the proper
closure of the work.

of specifically organized quasi-time. It is in this sense atemporal or supratemporal, and for this very reason it may be performed at any time, since it neither assumes a past nor postulates a future.

The time immanent in the musical work cannot be separated from the sound saturation of the work's specific moments because it is designated by the work and has in it its ontic base. These moments are made up of sound-constructs of various units of musical meaning.[13] A particularly important role in the formation of the work's temporal structure is played by rhythm and tempo, as well as by dynamic properties. A high speed, together with a suitably chosen rhythm, leads to a particular type of temporal organization in the work, not merely to its shorter duration in performance. Thus a stormy, passionate *presto* has a shorter duration, not only for the reason that, although the number of bars is the same, it does not last as long in performance as a solemn *adagio,* but most important because its speed entails greater concentration and tightening up of each wave of sound into a single phase, and these phases in their swift succession are transformed into a temporal totality of great intensity and concentration;[14] but a *largo* or a *lento* develops broadly in all its details and allows clear temporal accents in the slowly

13. This is my rendering of H. Riemann's "Sinnerheit" in his *Elemente der musikalischen Ästhetik.* See also W. Conrad, *Der ästhetische Gegenstand.*

14. S. Ossowski in his *The Foundations of Aesthetics* [*U podstaw estetyki,* Warsaw, 1933–ed.] is right when he says that "our impression that it is not the division of time which is changed but that time itself has begun to course more slowly or more quickly" (p. 28). But this remark, which is not based on an analysis of the temporal structure of the work, loses its value the more since its formulation leads us to think that what is involved is some "subjective experience" that the listener may or may not feel, depending on circumstances, but not a characteristic detail of the work itself. It is, however, such detail that I have in mind.

flowing phases and divisions. In all these cases, the very type of temporal structure is different; time is differently organized.

In view of all this, what is meant by the "supratemporality" of a musical work? It means only that the organized succession of the work's phases is in its coloring and organization, designated solely by the elements of the work itself and not by something that belongs to the real world outside the work. The quasi-temporal structure of a musical work is, so to speak, insensible to everything that exists outside of it. If we wish to change the work, we have to alter its sound-constructs.[15] This, of course, does not exclude the possibility that a work owes its origin to something outside, existing in the real world in a specified period of historical time. But this is a separate matter, which lies outside the analysis of a musical work's structure.

Both its supratemporality and its quasi-temporal structure remove the musical work from the real world and give it a self-contained character. In its content the work is completely separate from all other musical works, as well as from all nonmusical real objects. But in order not to be misunderstood in what I have just said, I must make several reservations.

As I have already stated, a performance of a work forms an element in the reality of everyday life and is in many ways dependent on surrounding circumstances, whereas the musical work as such, once it has been composed, is not dependent on those surroundings, nor does it possess any real sur-

---

15. If there were no scores or any other method of fixing a musical composition, then small changes and deviations from the work during performance and incorporated into future performances would interfere with the internal structure of the work and hence with the temporal structure. The musical score is a safeguard but whether it is completely adequate is discussed below in connection with a musical work's identity.

roundings at all.[16] There is probably no other type of art in which the work constitutes a distinct totality so perfectly self-contained as pure music, that is, music not associated with a literary text or containing representational or expressive elements. There is nothing in its content that refers to the real world. If we exclude all representational art where we can speak of this kind of reference, the art we may invoke as bearing comparison with the music on this account is architecture. Every architectural work—a church or palace—is connected with reality, not only because its material is a building which forms the ontic base of the architectural work (it is real and belongs to the real world) but also because its structure is such that this connection is essential. Every architectural work has or rather must have foundations, not only because the building which forms the work's ontic base would otherwise collapse, but because the work itself as a formation of solid masses (and not just as a certain geometric shape) postulates "rooting" on a given site. Such roots are normally invisible; nevertheless, they form part of this type of work. Moreover, the work's role is to stand in a specific area of real space, to be illuminated in a given way, to be visible from given vantage points. Its "weight" plays a role both in its construction and in aesthetic perception. Its construction must obey the laws of statics. Were these to be broken, the building would collapse and its aesthetic value might be affected. The work's structure emerges also from the phenomenally given palpable qualities of the material and the conditions in which it is to be perceived. We know that certain styles (e.g., the Gothic style) emerged from a solution of purely technical and practical problems. All this

16. This will upset all those who are incapable of perceiving a work of art other than as an aspect of the composer's biography. Whether the composer constitutes the musical work's "surroundings" is a matter I discuss below.

confirms that there is a real connection between the architectural work of art and the surrounding real world, irrespective of the existential character that we eventually ascribe to a work of architecture.

This connection is of course even clearer in all products of applied art. The bottom of a Greek wine jar is rounded rather than flat because, as we know, the Greeks placed these jars in the sand. It is sufficient to recall applied art theorists who regarded the adjustment of the work's composition to its purpose as the cardinal condition of its aesthetic value. Some (like A. Riegl) attempt, rightly or wrongly, to base general aesthetics on the connection of a work of art with its purpose and with the conditions in which it finds itself in the real world; they have chiefly in mind architecture and applied art. It is only when these theorists attempt to generalize their theory that they go too far.

This connection is also apparent in sculpture. Works of sculpture normally have a plinth. A view widely held by aestheticians is that the plinth performs a function analogous to that of a picture frame, that it separates the sculpture from the surrounding world in order to help the spectator to grasp the distinct wholeness of the work. I do not wish to contradict this view, but it is also true that the plinth is necessary because the piece of sculpture must stand on something. Moreover, sculpture always represents somatic or psychosomatic objects. The meaning of what is represented demands that the sculpture be placed somewhere in space and on some base, thus having its own space in which to stand. Finally, the conditions under which a work of sculpture is to be perceived—the vantage point and the distance from which it is to be viewed—influence the outline of its composition and again relate it to real surroundings. Moreover, we must not forget that all representational art refers to the real world in that, although the presented objects merely pretend to be real, they are always more or less faithful representations of

certain nonartistic real objects. This simulation of real objects is also one way in which a work of art refers to the real
world.

Only in pure music (which in any event is not the only
type of music) is there no reference whatever to the real
world. The world of sound-constructs and the edifices built
upon them forms a distinct realm. Every work forms an
ideally self-contained whole, not related to the real world
either through its sound material, through the gestalt of
sound-constructs of a higher order, or through its quasi-
temporal structure. Only where a composition begins to express something, as is the intention in program music, or
where the music-construct is to represent something that
itself is not a musical product, does the question arise as to
what type of connection, if any, is being realized between the
musical and the real world. I shall be considering this problem shortly.

The fact that not all music is expressive or representational,
without at the same time ceasing to be music, is perhaps the
best proof that the connection sometimes appearing between
the musical work and the real world is not an essential factor
for the musical composition. We may even doubt whether
such connections do contribute anything of musical value.
One feels that the supporters of pure music are right in this
respect, although they do forget the existence of impure music whose impurity does not necessarily diminish its value.
They are wrong, however, when they insist that in a musical
work there is nothing that is not in itself a sound-construct.
To this matter I shall now turn.

5

The Sounding and Nonsounding
Elements and Moments
of a Musical Work

As I have said, the musical work is a multiphased structure in which the basic[1] and elementary phenomena are sounding or rustling (percussive) qualities.[2]

It is upon these or from these that sound-constructs are erected that either span a single phase (moment) of a musical work or spread over a series of its phases. Sometimes, where the construction is particularly compact, they form within the work a temporal unit of a higher order. These constructs are ordered in such a way that in performance they *follow each other,* in the strict sense of the word, therefore acquiring various dependent temporal and qualitative characteristics. Thanks to these qualities, the sound-constructs constitute one totality, albeit one that is either more or less compactly organized and has various parts and qualities. The chain of sound-constructs does not exhaust the work's constitution,

---

1. They are basic in a dual sense: (a) Without them there could be no performance revealing the musical work as such; they therefore make the work's existential base possible in performance. (b) The totalities constructed from or upon them are such that through their synthetic shape shine simpler structures that constitute the evident foundation of these totalities.

2. Normally we simply talk of sounds, but this is inaccurate in that we can speak of sounds only in relation to a *performance* of a musical work.

for there are also various nonsounding qualities and constructs evidently superimposed upon the constructs. These
are designated by the work's sound foundation. It is when
sound-constructs combine with nonsounding ones that a fully constituted totality is created. I shall devote some intro-
ductory remarks to both these aspects of the musical work.

I The Sound Foundation of a Musical Composition

The sound-constructs that manifest themselves in the
work are—as I observed—fully constituted and concrete.
Apart from their strictly particular, unrepeatable elements,
they are characterized by certain general designations.[3] These
enable us to give a general description of the constructs and
classify them according to certain types.

In view of the varying complexity of the sound-constructs,
we distinguish various motifs, phrases, and subjects, which
form the elements of large sections of a musical work such as
the four movements of a sonata or symphony.[4] These constructs are distinguished from one another by varying de-
grees of sharpness. If the constructs are in themselves to constitute totalities, they must be distinguished one from the
other in direct perception—that is, a listener's—to an extent such that without special analysis one can hear where
one unit ends and another begins. This must happen not only where the units succeed each other immediately but also

3. The more original the work, the more marked is the presence of
unique qualities in the sound-constructs that make it up.
4. In what way these constructs of various orders may themselves be
totalities, in what way these totalities combine, and finally, in what way
the "large" sections of, say, a sonata are capable of forming a *single* musical
work, is one of the major problems concerning the totality of a musical
work.

where one passes into the other in such a way that a later sound-construct presents itself to the listener more or less clearly as a continuation of an earlier one. Where this feature is absent, we normally perceive it as a fault in the musical composition, unless the omission presents itself as characteristic and intentional. Only large sections, like movements of a sonata, are so separated from each other that there is no transition from one movement to the next. The duration of such a break[5] is not even measured with reference to the work's own time-scale.[6]

As a basis for these constructs of varying order and structure, there appear, as I remarked earlier, specific sounds. Although it is not true that such constructs consist simply of these, the sounds are nevertheless present in the totality of a construct to such an extent that their role in the formation of the given constructs does not vanish from the listener's perceptual field, even though he need not direct attention specifically to them. But, because in the stream of sound-constructs they are somehow noticed (heard), the result, at least in certain cases, is the phenomenon of "movement," chiefly melodic, but in other cases constructs, which we call "chords." It is not that, as the associationists used to say, we first perceive individual sounds and tones, which in a separate process we then combine or weave into the totality of a musical composition; this is confirmed by the fact that when we hear a chord or a melody, we often cannot even tell what individual sounds it comprises. Only people with perfect

5. Here, as everywhere, we have exceptions: for example, the transition between the third and last movement of Beethoven's Fifth Symphony.
6. On the other hand, the so-called pauses within a particular part, or even within a single musical composition, do form an element of the work measured in terms of the given part of the work. Especially when they appear within a sound-construct, they form its necessary element and are characteristic of its structure.

pitch or with special musical training are capable of this. The listener hears the sounds that form part of a musical composition only incidentally; his attention is directed chiefly toward constructs of a higher order—to motifs, melodies, chords, and chord-clusters.

Musical compositions always display a specific assortment of evident properties that to some extent are hierarchically ranged. They play a greater or lesser role in the totality of a given composition. Some of them come to the fore and stamp the composition with a homogeneous quality; they constitute its "nature." Others belong to it only as approximate characterizations or even secondary colorings. Musicologists sometimes call these various traits or aspects of musical compositions the "elements" of a work. Thus J. M. Chomiński writes in his *Formy muzyczne:* "The elements of music include melodics, agogics, dynamics, and colorings." In fact, it is the specific and *concrete musical structures* that constitute these elements, and it is they that possess various properties of melody, rhythm, harmony, agogics, dynamics, and coloring. Where the melodic properties are particularly prominent, where they characterize the totality of the composition, giving it a specific dominant shape (constituting the qualitative determination of its nature), then the given, concrete composition, which is also determined in various ways by properties of the other types mentioned, is a fully determined melody. It has its own melodic line, rhythm, characteristic tempo, constant or varying volume, and coloring. Sometimes a melody develops upon a complex harmonic base. The melody then weaves itself through a changing sound field, constructed harmonically, thus acquiring in its specific phases a number of dependent secondary colorings, designated by the simultaneous appearance of the melody's certain phase and the harmonically organized sound environment. As long as the melody dominates the sound-cluster, it also becomes the axis of the particular fragment of the work (e.g., of a subject) and often emerges changed and varied. The residue of sound forms the environment, performing in relation to it a subservient note of secondary coloring. By contrast, at other times harmonic properties dominate the sound-cluster and stamp the qualitative unity upon the work or its fragment. The main element of the work then consists of the harmonic sound-construct through which a melodic line may weave itself but incidentally, now merely completing, enriching, and ornamenting the developing harmonic composition in which, apart from the weaving melody, properties of rhythm, tempo, and volume also appear.

Finally, it is also possible for the musical composition to be dominated by a rhythm, for while melodic, harmonic, and other properties appear in such a sound work, they play a rather subservient role in determining the totality. In extreme cases these subservient properties fade and vanish completely, leaving a purely rhythmical work, such as African ritual compositions for drums. On the other hand, neither dynamic properties nor tempo nor the choice of sound colorings can constitute the main element of a musical composition.[7] They merely provide supplementary determination of musical works.[8]

A certain temporally arranged amalgam of succeeding musical constructs, passing one into another, form what

7. This does not rule out the case where the choice of the work's sound pigmentation (the coloring) may for aesthetic reasons play a dominant role in the work and determine its worth. But this does not turn the choice into a constitutive element of the work alongside the musical constructs I have enumerated.

8. Musicologists are right in calling melody, rhythm, and harmony the basic elements and the three remaining properties secondary—though I do not favor the term "element."

may be called the base of a musical work. When we have to do with a work of art as an aesthetic object and not just as a complex acoustic signal, the musical work is not confined to its sound base, for it is only on this base that the nonsounding elements are built up, partly woven or melted into that base, partly superimposed upon it, partly subordinated to it. Let us now move on to a sketchy consideration of these various types.

II The Nonsounding Elements of a Musical Work

To begin with, we have to acknowledge that existing musical works differ greatly as to whether and to what extent they contain elements that are not of a purely sounding nature. Some works are devoid of these elements; in others a large number of them have a considerable role. Thus, although the elements may be of great significance in these works and may even at times determine their value, they are not essential to *all kinds* of musical works just because they do not appear in all of them. Whether works in which elements do not appear are thereby deprived of one aspect of their value as works of art or aesthetic objects is a question concerning not the structure of the works but their value. In analyzing structure, we must consider not only works of great value but also inferior works and even those of no value at all. Even bad music is still music and not just an agglomeration of acoustic phenomena.

For simplicity's sake I shall consider only works of comparatively rich structure in order to discover, if possible, all the types of nonsounding elements appearing in musical works. I will discuss them successively according to the closeness of their connection with the sound-constructs of the musical work.

1. If we agree that rhythm and tempo constitute only

those aspects of sound-constructs that, while in themselves not sounds nevertheless directly give rise to certain features flowing out of and characteristic of sounds,[9] then the first nonsounding element of a musical work closely connected with the properties of sound-constructs although not characteristic of them, is the work's temporal or quasi-temporal structure. This I have already discussed. Now I wish to demonstrate that this structure itself is nonsounding although it does flow out of the properties of sound-constructs. This structure is not confined to the simple fact that specific sounds or sound-constructs forming part of the work have a designated duration and that they follow one another in a determined order that consists chiefly in the sequence of qualitative variants in the passing of the time-phases of the work itself and in the type of temporal elements in the work, all of which I have called the organization of time[10] in a musical work. It may manifest itself differently in different works or even in different parts of the same work. The variations of structure are connected principally with the properties of tempo and rhythm that happen to dominate the given phase of the work or the work as a whole but specific melodic properties also may play their part. Differences may depend on the shape of movement of the melodic line and on sound-constructs of a higher order, whereas the properties of harmony, although they influence the temporal coloring of specific temporal elements of the work, play a lesser role

9. Some interpret the phenomenon of rhythm so widely that according to them it is also present in nonmusical works like architecture and includes the "rhythm" of arches and vaults. Although this may be analogous to rhythm in music, it is surely not quite the same thing.

10. Musicologists tell me that Stravinsky also used this concept, but I have not been able to trace the evidence. If this information is accurate, and we both have introduced this concept quite independently, it would be an interesting indication that both of us were relying on certain data of musical experience.

in coordinating the organization of the work's time span in its elements.[11] In this structured duration of the work, there appears not only the purely sound aspect but also everything that manifests itself in the work. Conversely the temporal coloring of the specific moments, as well as the types of time-flow, play a large role in the constitution both of the emotional qualities in the musical work (more about this below) and in the aesthetic values proper to the given work.

Every musical work manifests time structured in some way or other but time is not only characteristic of music as such, for it is also present in all multiphased works of art, most notably in literature, film, and drama.

2. Another nonsounding element of a musical work is movement. It is most closely linked with sounds and their clusters, and it manifests itself in the development of sound-clusters like musical runs. On the one hand, it is a phenomenon specifically of motion and therefore, contrary to what is sometimes said, cannot be identified simply with the change in the sound-construct when new sounds appear. On the other hand, neither is it motion in the strict sense, that is of a change of position in space.[12] It is a quite specific "motion" that accompanies the development of some musical constructs. We apprehend it in a purely auditory manner

11. This ought to be analyzed on the basis of the given musical material, but I must confine myself to general remarks. In 1949 G. Brelet published a two-volume *Temps musical,* in which she gave a detailed analysis of musical time. She has undoubtedly solved some problems, but her arguments are often none too clear.

12. Not every change connected with the appearance of new sounds leads to "motion" in music. Thus, for example, purely harmonic changes in a sequence of chords do not by themselves entail the phenomenon of motion. We have to speak of musical motion principally where a melody unfolds itself. Naturally enough, the properties of rhythm and tempo play a large role in the manifestation of movement and in the definition of its properties.

when we perceive the formation in time of the work's melody. Where there are several voices unfolding simultaneously, as in a Bach fugue, we hear also a number of concurrent motions. This motion takes place in the qualitative time of a musical work and at the same time influences the work's organization. Further, it moves in tandem with yet another nonsounding element of a musical work, namely, with the peculiar musical space that has nothing to do with the real, perceived, or imagined space of, say, the hall in which the concert is being performed. This space constitutes itself through the multiplicity of motions of the developing musical constructs. We could almost say that we can hear this space when we listen to the progressing musical constructs, although we may doubt whether it would be proper to speak directly of an auditory space, of *Höreraum,* as some German writers put it. It is, however, the case that in hearing the space phenomenally called up by motion in music we often associate with it an imagined visual space, particularly when representational elements appear in the work. This imagined visual space is not rigorously related to the patterns of sounds or sound-clusters that form part of the musical work, but merely belongs to it, assuming this is really justified by the representational elements of the work. On the other hand, the space that constitutes itself in the work in the multiplicity of motions of the sound-constructs is strictly bound up with the shape of those motions; it is designated by them as the specific medium in which they occur—a medium that is analogous to the given musical work's own time.[13]

13. Naturally I have in mind the state of affairs in pure musical works devoid of literary texts that might suggest extra-musical dimensions. Undoubtedly, things are different in works consisting of a musical composition and a literary text (as in opera and songs) but the situation there is complex and demands separate analysis. What we must not do is transfer the state of affairs that is manifest in such complex works to compositions of pure music. Space in music is discussed by E. Furth in *Musikpsychologie.*

The phenomenon of motion in music is inseparable from musical constructs that have a clear melodic line and temporal development. It is of great significance to the manifestation within the work of further nonsounding elements, especially of emotional qualities, aesthetically valuable qualities, and the qualities of the aesthetic values themselves, which I shall discuss presently. Motion in music is, however, linked with the question of the continuity of the process of the specific fragments of the work and with the separation of some melodic sound-constructs from others. It distinguishes one melodic construct from others, which may be developing at the same time (from the whole sound background, for instance the accompaniment, or from other melodic voices developing simultaneously), or from sound-constructs that follow the given construct. A fugue, for instance, is distinguished by the several simultaneously developing motions of sound-constructs and is therefore marked by a complexity of the phenomenon of the motion of the whole. This phenomenon may constitute one of the specific aesthetically valuable qualities by which the work is distinguished. With a common tempo and rhythm of the interweaving motions, such a cluster of motions contributes to a clear organization of time.

Where there is a division between two distinct successive melodic constructs, the motion of the former either breaks off sharply or gently turns the phenomenon into the motion of the latter. There is also the phenomenon of the breakup of a motion that commences but is incapable of effective development because, although scarcely begun, it is cut short unexpectedly; it is then succeeded by a different motion not linked with the former and just as unexpectedly broken off. A specific disharmony of motion results, accompanied by a specific anxiety, since the sound-constructs in whose development such uncoordinated and disrupted motions appear do not themselves reach an effective development and constitution. They are seemingly *in statu nascendi* incomplete, broken off, and stunted. They fail to link up with other sound-constructs that follow them. The work acquires the character of *disjecta membra*. It becomes unclear why a particular section should be followed by another. It is difficult to decide whether we have now reached the borderline between a musical work and a sequence of uncoordinated sounds or whether we have here a specific type of musical work. The fact that this kind of question may arise shows what a significant role is played in the structure of a musical work by the motion designated by the choice of sound-constructs. Even the phenomenon of motionlessness or calm constitutes only an appendage to the phenomenon of motion in music and joins the totality of the phenomena of movement in the given work as their specific completion. It is significant that "movement" is used to designate sections of musical work.

3. The "forms" of specific musical constructs (e.g., the shape of a melodic line and the constitution of harmonic constructs, including the structure of specific chords) are also nonsounding in nature even though they manifest themselves directly as the determinants of sound-constructs. These "forms" are heterogeneous and like the sound-constructs are of ascending order, culminating in the "form" of the work as a whole. These forms may be either strictly individual—peculiar to the given work—or general—characteristic of many works—and yet more or less schematic, so that in each specific work they must be supplemented by further formal elements. We may, however, consider whether one and the same fully articulated form may appear in two different concrete sound-constructs; that is, for example, the "same" melody as far as form is concerned but having as its base different concrete sounds: i.e., sounds occurring at different pitches or keys or even played upon different instruments and therefore possessing different colorings. Now we

undoubtedly have to distinguish an absolutely concrete and individualized "form" appearing in a *single* sounding construct from a form that is abstracted yet fully articulated (even built on the basis of identical notes but appearing in different phases of the same work) and able to be reiterated in several musical constructs. These constructs are different if only because, when they appear in different phases of the same work, they have secondary, dependent, qualitative determinations arising from their different positions in the temporal sequence of the work, while their recurring abstract "form" remains exactly the same. This repeatability seems to constitute the essence of musical "forms," forms that strictly speaking are not "forms" in the sense of formal ontology but rather "qualities" of a specific kind (we normally call them "shaping qualities"). Their specific "formalism" is characterized by the fact that their concrete sound-base may within certain limits be different while their identity is retained.[14] If the same form is to be preserved, what cannot be changed in its base is the relative pitch of the succeeding sounds and their order in the domain of the same musical sound-construct.

A great variety of musical "forms" exists, and we cannot consider them all in detail.[15] Two things are of importance to us now. First, the "forms" of sound-constructs in the present sense are not themselves sounds or even a collection or

14. Here we face various difficult ontological problems whose solution would make it possible to clarify the nature of "form," which is our concern here, but it seems to me that this is not essential for reaching an understanding with my readers and would lead us into unnecessarily general and abstract reasoning.

15. Important at this stage is a clear distinction between sound-construct and its "form," for musicologists often tend to coalesce these two concepts in such a way that by a musical form they mean nothing more than the sound-construct, whereas here "form" means a specific, dependent element of the sound-construct.

selection of sounds but rather a selection or collection of the special, sound-dependent elements of these sounds. The fact that these elements cannot be separated from the totality of the sounding construct, except by abstraction, does not in any way alter their specific nonsounding character. It is of course possible to assume that each dependent element constituting the determination of sounding construct is itself a sounding element, but this does not seem to be correct. We must not overlook the fact that the musical forms referred to here are not the forms of simple sounding elements of a work but are always the structures of *compound* constructs, or rather constructs of a higher order, which at their base have a certain *multiplicity* of sounds. From this point of view, it is natural that musical forms as structures of this type are not in themselves any longer sounding determinants of musical constructs.

The other point is that musical forms constitute in a musical work an agent of rational ordering. It is first of all striking that these "forms," particularly the basic ones, either do or can recur over and over again in the same work, either in an identical shape or transformed in such a way that the strong resemblance of recurring forms is manifest. In literature, this phenomenon is known only in poetry as, say, a verse pattern, an arrangement of verses in a sonnet, or a rhyming scheme. It is not only unheard of in other literary genres but is in fact quite foreign to the structure of the literary work as such. Where it does appear, we experience it precisely as a *musical* element in literature, and, in any event, it appears principally in the sound layer of a literary work. If, for example, in Homer certain phrases and expressions recur as refrains accompanying given situations, we must not forget that the *Iliad* was originally sung, and this points to a musical source for these repetitions. But in music, especially older and classical music, the repetition of certain basic forms is a constant feature and belongs to the principles of composition. In modern music, the repetition of basic forms is rather the exception. It is precisely in this that modern music differs radically from older music. If the recurrence of basic forms does not initiate, it at least underlies forcefully the "ordering" role of musical forms in a musical work. We may say that there is a certain specific "geometry" of musical forms that brings into the heterogeneity of a musical work a number of necessary norms regarding the copresence, succession, and specific hierarchy of layered forms. These necessary norms can be not only discovered but also understood, and this also goes for their specific application in particular works. Hence, the quality in them that constitutes a particular order in the musical work introduces into the totality of the work a certain rationality, and in particular a *rational perspicuity,* into the work's structure. Such perspicuity does not exclude the presence of emotional qualities. On the contrary, Bach's "classical" music is characterized not only by a high degree of rationality in construction and a hierarchy of mutually entwined musical forms, but also by the clearly discernible emotional and even metaphysical qualities. The basic forms of Bach's music already display something outstandingly rational, and the same goes for the very rhythmically ordered organization of time within his compositions. Only through this rational ordering do we glimpse the full depth of the emotional, irrational element. There is no doubt that in Romantic music the element of rational ordering is subdued, while the role of emotional qualities is intensified. These emotional qualities do not emerge from behind the strict order in which the elementary forms recur. They in fact appear directly in the melodic expansiveness, the dynamic violence, the fluctuations of the temporal organization (*rubato*), and the choice of colorings of simultaneously developing contrasting sound-constructs, as in Tchaikovsky's symphonies. Yet the ordering agent does not disappear but seems to hide behind all the phenomena as an essential agent in European music.

In so-called modern music the agent of rational ordering cannot so easily be grasped, and its role in the construction of a work is the more difficult to appreciate. Among the representatives and champions of modern music we would undoubtedly find both those who regard it as the most "rationalized" music and those who regard it as a flowering of irrationality. Before arriving at a position here we would have to carry out a more detailed analysis that would penetrate deeper into the construction of modern works. The tendency to avoid the reiteration of basic forms, particularly of higher-order forms, is worth pondering. On the other hand, there is a striking diminution of emotional qualities. One could say especially that some modern musical works are "cold," or at least foreign to that expansive, exuberant emotionalism so characteristic of "Romantic" music. Both facts may play a certain role in the consideration of the type and degree of rationality or irrationality in "modern" musical works.[16] In any event, I do not wish to arrive at a definite conclusion, and the problem has only a marginal interest for our inquiry into the nonsounding elements of musical works.

4. From what I have just said, it will be clear that I recognize the existence of emotional qualities within a musical work. They appear upon specific sound-constructs, both of a higher and of a lower order, and sometimes they permeate the whole of the work in a characteristic way. In "emotional qualities" I include both purely emotional "feeling" qualities and qualities of desires, states of excitement, satisfaction,

---

16. "Modern music" is a very loose term because there are great differences among the works to which the term is applied. This fact makes it more difficult to solve the problem I have here indicated.

and exultation. When we take "emotional qualities" in this wide sense we detect their presence in many musical works. Sometimes even the coloring of a sound carries a specific emotional character, as in, say, the opening bars of Tchaikovsky's *Pathétique Symphony*. This is true even more of motifs and musical constructs of a higher order, such as, for example, all the melodic qualities in Chopin's works. There are practically no musical compositions that lack emotional qualities. In fact these qualities are varied and tend to dominate the work.

Again, these qualities are not of a sounding character, but at the same time they are so closely connected to sound-constructs that, as a result, they themselves seem to undergo deep modification. They are exclusive to music and only *resemble* properties appearing, say, in a landscape or in the appearance of a living human face under emotional stress. Having these last qualities in mind, and not distinguishing them sufficiently from the emotional qualities appearing in the content of musical works (understanding them as certain aesthetic objects), it is mistakenly said of these emotional qualities (admittedly peculiar to music) that they constitute "extra-musical subjects." For despite all their similarity to the qualities that appear either as determinants of particular psychic states or processes or as evident features of real objects given (for example, in perception but not having anything to do with music), the emotional qualities in musical works are so specifically merged with sound-constructs that this is reflected in their coloring in a way not found anywhere outside music. We may therefore conclude that they are *specifically musical*, emotional qualities possessing such force and dynamic presence that they are more "affective" than in any of the other arts. It is as if in the outline of a certain melody (with the cooperation of the sound-coloring forming its base), "sweetness," "sadness," or "melancholy" were to appear. In the very harmonic cluster of certain selections of succeeding chords there is a palpably visible "seriousness" (cf. Chopin's Prelude No. 20, Op. 28), "terror," or "anxiety."[17]

Emotional qualities need not manifest themselves in every musical work nor in every phase of a work in which they are present. We have simply to ascertain their presence in an objective way. Only then should we raise the question as to how this came about, assuming anyone finds this strange. In considering this question, we must not be guided by theoretical prejudices arising from supposedly scientifically "determined" theses regarding the fundamental difference between so-called sensible qualities,[18] the sounding ones in particular, and emotional qualities—a difference that is supposed to be so radical that it is "impossible" for, say, color

---

17. These words are too general and do not convey the specific character of, say, terror in a musical work in contrast with terror in a landscape threatened by a heavy storm. Language, especially scientific language, is meager in its terminology designating various emotional qualities that we distinguish precisely enough in direct experience but have great difficulty in distinguishing linguistically. Attention to this has been drawn by Stefan Szuman.

18. Nineteenth-century psycho-physiology has identified these "sensible" qualities that appear in people's daily experience as *qualifications of real objects* (e.g., trees, stones, and houses) with "sensible experiences," which each one of us experiences separately in sense perception. It has interpreted them as a specific product of a sense-organ. Following J. Müller in accepting the distinctiveness of sense-energy, for example, of hearing, and its isolation from other physiologic/anatomic factors (thanks to which we experience emotional qualities), nineteenth-century psychology arrived at the thesis that there apparently is a fundamental distinction between sensible and emotional qualities and did not allow them to appear together as elements of a totality. It is further assumed that when we experience a musical work, we use only the organ of hearing, and this, together with the assumptions already outlined, leads to the conclusion that only "impressions" (the sound data) may emerge in the field of our experience—that if we think there also arise emotional qualities, this is simply an illusion since nothing of this sort can be thus given. Those who argue thus, forgetting that they have already accepted that these sound data

are only "sensible impressions," now contrast sounds as being something "objective" to emotional qualities as only "subjective psychic content." The next step is to treat this content as our "psychic reaction" to "music," which, on this interpretation, reverts to being something "objective" and thus regains the character proper to it in immediate experience, a character which these psycho-physiologists treating sounds as "sense impressions" now deny. If, however, we do not identify "sense impressions" (or, more accurately, the "experiential auditory or visual data") with qualities given to us in direct perception as qualifications of physical objects, if we also do not identify the concretely heard sounds of a musical work with the sound-constructs of the musical work itself, if we also reject the isolation (which has no basis in reality) of the sense-organ from other anatomico-physiological elements of the nervous system (on all of which probably the appearance of emotional qualities in experience depends), we shall not see any difficulty in remaining faithful to experience and accepting the merging *in concreto* of those qualities with sound qualities. And only on this basis will we ask what the connections are between the various parts of our nervous system and the mental functions associated with them that allow the constitution of such a perception of a musical work in a specific performance so that both the categories or qualities appear there in the strictest coordination and have the same existential character. Either they are both elements of the same object, namely a musical work apprehended in aesthetic experience, or both these categories are equally "subjective." But psychic "content" is accessible in internal perception (in the so-called reflection), whereas no one listens to a musical work on the basis of a specific performance in such a way that he undergoes an act of "intro-spection" or of "internal perception." Perhaps, therefore, we should aban-don the view that the qualities of both the categories are psychic material ("impressions," etc.) and agree that they constitute specific qualifications of the aesthetic object whose existence is conditioned on the one hand by the listener performing certain perceptual acts, and, on the other hand, by the real occurrence of a performance of the given work on the basis of which the work itself is revealed with all its heterogeneous qualifications. We may agree to this conditioning without negating the data of our im-mediate experience, and the acceptance of this conditioning does not in any way undermine any of the claims about a musical work that I have tried to present. For this conditioning says only that the musical work given in aesthetic perception on the basis of certain perception is not a real object, and this precisely is the thesis that I am here trying to establish. As to what existential character we may positively assign to a musical work, this is a matter to which I shall return.

qualities and qualities of feeling and desire to appear jointly within a concrete totality. I think that we must first, without prejudice, ascertain the facts as they appear in direct experience and only then seek to explain them in relation to processes and sense organs, so that, given a reality independent of the listener, there should emerge amid the data of experience just those objects with just those qualifications. It is these facts that controvert the thesis that it is impossible for sound and emotional qualities to appear together, in the sense here presented, as a single concrete totality.

In order to ascertain objectively the presence of emotional qualities in a musical work concretized in performance, we have to attain a still more accurate analysis of experience not blurred with faulty a priori interpretations. We have, that is, to distinguish the emotional qualities rooted in the sounding material of the musical sound-constructs from feelings that the listener might experience under the influence of the work he is hearing; that is, from the feelings either that are aroused by the performance or with which he responds to the performance. We must also distinguish these emotional qualities from feelings experienced through the work performed in concreto by an interpreter. These expressed feelings may be in turn feelings of the performer, moved by the work he is performing[19] or of the composer—Bach, Beethoven, or Chopin—experienced during the composition of the work.

In a particular instance it is comparatively difficult to distinguish the feeling qualities appearing in the work itself and designated by the properties of the sound-constructs constituting the work from the feelings of the composer or

19. This of course makes sense only if there is a single performer—a Petri or a Rubinstein. When the work is performed by a hundred-piece orchestra, the feelings of individual players do not come to the surface, although sometimes the whole ensemble may develop a common feeling that may be reflected in the "expression" of the work being performed.

interpreter expressed through the work in a specific performance. The former admittedly manifest themselves as a
concrete, evident phenomenon in the work itself (e.g., Chopin's *Revolutionary Etude*) as a dependent determination of
the sound-constructs themselves, whereas the latter *shine*
through the work and are never presented to us as directly as
the former. At the same time, the former play a significant
role in the shining-through of the latter and, moreover, in
the method of performance, and the interpreter's feelings
play a part in the realization of a given work. In this way,
there may come about an exchange of influences between the
emotional qualities of the work and the feelings of either
composer or interpreter, so that the clear distinction between them is blurred and the listener arrives at his expressed feelings through perceiving the emotional qualities
of a work in performance. It is easy to mix the two types of
feelings and to draw false conclusions regarding the composer's feelings. Nevertheless, in listening to the same work
in several performances, the listener can contrast these various emotional experiences or at least distinguish them mentally, thus arriving at an awareness of the emotional qualities
in the work itself. Here it may be helpful to study the structure of the sound-constructs of a given work with the aid of
the score, although a critical listener will find it comparatively easy to distinguish between the emotional qualities
manifest in the work and his own feelings experienced while
listening to the performance. The listener's emotions—
the mental state or the process that he undergoes and that
"moves" him—are all his own, whereas the emotional qualities manifest themselves in something in his presence that he
finds among the data of musical experience. The listener,
too, experiences his feelings as something taking place in
himself, often realizing that this is happening because he is in
the presence of a work of music and the emotional qualities

that are manifest in it. It is with them that he is in direct
contact. Sometimes he observes these emotional qualities
dispassionately; sometimes he succumbs to them, and having thus become infected, he may internally approve them so
that his emotional state becomes one of wonder. But sometimes, on the contrary, he rejects these qualities, repudiating
them in a new emotional state and condemning them for one
reason or another.[20] There are also occasions when the listener, having succumbed to the work's influence and fallen
into a particular emotional state, seems passively to trans-
pose his feelings on to the work, perceiving the work under a
particular emotional aspect, ascribing to it a succession of
emotional qualities that are alien to it and therefore falsify it.
The danger of this happening is possible in both the situations I have distinguished, but it is relatively more serious
where the listener's emotional state is in conflict with the
emotional qualities of the work. At the same time it is precisely this conflict that proves most conclusively the presence
of emotional qualities in the work itself. We may, for instance, begin listening to a work in a cheerful state but perceive in the work an emotion of despair (at odds with our
cheerfulness) by which we become affected, as if infected,
finally rejecting it in a clearly negative, emotional reaction.
Such facts also stand against the fairly common view that in
every case emotional qualities manifesting themselves in a
musical work (or any other art) are merely a "projection" of
the listener's own feelings on to the work or its fragments—
the "empathy" (*Einfühling*) between the listener's feelings

20. This is neither theory nor "metaphysics" but an accurate description of what happens to a listener during his perception of a musical work.
Similar factors operate during the perception of other types of art. It is
with analysis and description of these factors that we begin our investigation into the modes of the observer's communion with a work of art.

and something in itself emotionally neutral.[21] The appearance of emotional qualities in a musical work would then seem to be caused by an illusion falsifying the work's true nature. This would be understandable where there is a consonance between the listener's emotions and the emotional qualities appearing in musical works, but the empathy theory would not be able to explain instances of conflict between the two emotional elements. Thus, although we have to admit that there are instances of the imposition of the listener's own feelings on to a musical work, nevertheless, these are not cases where the listener discovers and grasps the emotional qualities proper to the work itself but only instances of specific falsification of the work. There are, of course, people quite incapable of surrendering to the work and reading its peculiar and characteristic features, but the fact that such people exist does not compel us to treat their responses as a basis for a theory of the structure of a musical work or for a view regarding perception suitable for discovery of a work's properties.

5. When we talk of the emotions (or other mental states) of the composer or the performer that at times are expressed by the work or its performance, we must realize that we are moving beyond the work to something that in itself does not constitute any of the work's elements but can at best—given a work's special features—*belong* to it. If, during a particular performance (and given a proper sequence of perceptions) a particular work does exercise the function of expressing[22]

---

21. The empathy theory of aesthetic experience was fashionable at the turn of the century, and its main exponents within psychologistic aesthetics were Theodore Lipps and, to some extent, J. Volkelt.

22. Distinct from the problem of expression is the fact that we sometimes *infer* this or that about the properties or states of the composer on the basis of confirmed properties of the work. We often do this in art history and human psychology. Here we are liable to error because the subject of

the composer's or performer's feelings, then the work evidently imparts information about something other than itself, something which normally belongs to the real world.[23] This knowledge, though it does have an evident base in the work itself, may be false when applied to a specific real person. But in any event it takes us outside the work itself. We likewise move beyond the work when we focus on the feeling that a given work in a particular performance evokes in us as listeners. Neither the listener nor his experience (in particular his perception and feeling aroused by the work) constitute the elements or independent features of the work being heard, although it is true that in certain cases the occurrence of the feeling reflects on the shape in which the given work presents itself to the listener. It need not always lead to the falsification of the work, because the feeling aroused in the listener while perceiving the work may sometimes help to deepen the sense of the work's value and to improve its understandability. But in every instance any such feeling and the heard work are two totally distinct totalities.

6. We go outside the musical work in a somewhat different way when its "representational" themes (*Darstellungsmotive*) lead us to think or imagine the things presented by them. Such themes may be of different types and I am not here primarily concerned with for instance, Wagner's leitmotifs (e.g., "Wotan's leitmotif" or "Brünnhilde's leitmotif") for as such they are not representational. Had we not known from the text of the opera that a given leitmotif re-

---

our inference does not reveal itself in the work of art, and the connection between the properties of the work and the properties of mental states of the composer is on the whole neither perspicuous nor unambiguous.

23. I say "normally" because a closer analysis reveals that "author" is ambiguous and that only in one of its meanings does it designate a specific real person, namely, the creator of the work.

presents Wotan, the musical shape alone would not have informed us of this. Yet, the fire theme in *Das Rheingold* does perform the function of representing through a certain resemblance with the subject. What concerns us are themes that lead us away from themselves and make us think of a more or less distinct object. If the object is real, the theme takes us out of the world of art altogether; if, however, it is meant to be imagined, although it may also belong to a type of real objects, then the representational theme leads us beyond the musical work as such to something extra-musical. Yet this extra-musical element *belongs* to the work thanks to the representational element and brings about a higher-level totality, made up of the musical work and those "represented" imagined objects. These two elements may even consist in a certain aesthetically valuable harmony. The kind of program music that eschews literary texts wishes to achieve, with the help of representational themes, precisely such a higher-level totality. This is the case with Debussy's symphonic poems and some of his piano pieces. Here the literary text, often confined to the title, is not required. Its role is taken over by the representational themes, by certain specifically arranged sound-constructs endowed with temporal structure, motion, emotional qualities, and normally by a characteristic sound form, which brings to mind certain objects. These constructs are sufficient in themselves for the intentional creation of the second, object-type element in this artistic totality. The fact that what is represented is burdened with a certain generality and indefiniteness and lacks both the precision and the conceptually designated content characteristic of objects represented in a literary work is not disputed but is also symptomatic of pure program music. Someone not satisfied with this may append a thematically determined title or even a full literary text, moving then beyond pure music to the borderline between music and literature. This is the domain of songs, operas, and Wagnerian music drama in which the function of representing objects constitutes itself only in small degree by musical representational elements, the emphasis being on signifying linguistic constructs. But the perception of the work ceases to be purely "musical." It consists of heterogeneous elements, only one of which may be called musical perception, and this is not independent of the other elements.

The constructs presented in a piece of program music (without a literary text) may be called quasi-musical objects because they do belong to that type of musical composition but are not themselves "musical," if we accept them precisely in the way they are designated by the presentational themes. But they are not extra-musical, for if they were, they would either be objects designated and presented by linguistic means or real objects ontologically independent of the musical work, about which the listener, assuming a suitable attitude, may learn through the musical work itself—as, for example, when on the basis of the work he draws conclusions about the attributes of its author—matters about which he can be much better informed by quite different cognitive methods, e.g., in direct experience.

The presentational function of musical themes that represent without recourse to linguistic elements is in principle different from the presentational function performed in a literary work by linguistic constructs. Words, phrases, and sentences perform that function because they possess sense and carry meaningful thoughts. The sounds of words are carriers of semantic intentions. As such, they refer to certain objects (things, processes, and events) depending on their meaning-content, formally shaped and qualitatively endowed. Assuming sufficient precision in the meaning of a given linguistic construct, these objects are clearly distinguished with regard to their properties and ontological status. The representational themes of pure program music, however, are not linguistic constructs; they do not possess meanings characteristic of linguistic constructs, and the objects presented by them are not so sharply determined in their properties and their nature. How these themes can nevertheless represent something and thus designate some object—something in any event separate from them: the rustle of a stream, the thud of horses' feet, storm sounds, or Pelleas's cry of despair—is a complex problem and would demand separate treatment. Here I must content myself with the negative statement that there is a fundamental difference between the representational elements of program music and linguistic constructs, principally because the former represent mainly through resemblance to the objects being represented (hence the narrow range of objects that may be thus represented), whereas linguistic constructs do not call for any resemblance between the sound and meaning of the work and the presented object, nor would such resemblance aid language in its representational task. This distinction does become blurred to some extent in extreme and exceptional works such as certain onomatopoeic poems that are neither music nor literature in the strict sense.

7. Returning, however, to pure music, we discover one further nonsounding element that has the closest connection with musical works and manifests itself when such works already possess all the nonsounding elements already discussed. This element is made up of aesthetically valuable qualities and the qualities of aesthetic values. A detailed discussion of these qualities, especially demonstrating that there are specifically *musical* qualities of this type, would demand a separate study. Here I will confine myself to a few examples.

I begin with a general observation. In the time-honored dispute, stretching back to the Greeks, between the defenders of form and the defenders of content regarding what constitutes a work of art, people commit a fundamental error due to oversimplification of the problem.[24]

Discussions on the location of aesthetic value envisage a priori three, and only three possibilities: first, that only the formal elements of a work of art, its "form," are aesthetically valuable; second, that only the "content" (the material) is aesthetically valuable; or, third, that the value lies in a certain specific congruence (harmony) between form and content within a particular work.[25] This is how these positions are normally stated, although their proponents have something more far-reaching in mind. They assume, that is, that *all* the work's formal elements (all form) are aesthetically valuable, and those who talk of the work's "form" normally mean the totality of these elements. The same applies to the content theorists. It is thought sufficient to point either to the work's form or its content in order to discover its aesthetic value— hence the frequent attempts at establishing the form of a given work. The moment we lay bare this assumption, however, it becomes clear that it is false. In order to demonstrate this, we must first establish at least a general sense of form

24. There is one further view typical of all *skeptical* theories of value. This is that the work's value does not exist at all, that there is only a subjective emotional state or a so-called evaluation performed by the valuing subject that creates merely an appearance of the existence of values. According to this view, the work of art itself is a completely neutral construct. I cannot deal with this view here, especially since, like every skeptical theory, it is impervious to counterarguments and, despite its skepticism, is utterly self-confident and full of scorn for those who do not accept it. It usually resorts to accusations of "metaphysics" and "irrationality," placing itself on a pedestal of "rationality," objectivity, criticism, and sobriety. The skeptic is, however, very uncritical in relation to his own experiences of works of art, an attitude sometimes caused by lack of such experiences altogether and an inability to respond to works of art.

25. For the moment I ignore the fact that the respective defenders of these three views normally employ the unclarified concepts of "form" and "content" and in most cases use them in highly ambiguous fashion.

that can be applied to a work of art—in particular a musical work—and also to demonstrate in general and with reference to a specific case what this form is. These are among the problems that have not been settled by philosophical theorists of music. It is impossible here and now to carry through an investigation that would clarify the issue. Let us for the moment simplify the problem and assume that the forms of musical constructs and the forms of their composition into the totality of a musical work constitute the work's formal elements. Would we then agree that all these forms, and only these, constitute what is aesthetically valuable in a musical work? Is it not true that the artistic character of music depends on an ability to select from all such possible forms only those that might be aesthetically valuable? And is it not the case that among the forms so selected there stands out a group that is aesthetically valuable, while the rest are neutral with regard to value? And are there not aesthetically valuable elements in the work, apart from the forms of musical constructs?

It seems to me that one who assumed all formal elements and only formal elements to be aesthetically valuable would be doing so in order to simplify the problem and make its solution easier. A difficulty arises in the task of explaining what form is and what constitutes the form of a musical work. Now we have the additional difficulty of distinguishing those formal elements that are aesthetically valuable from those that are neutral or negative. Are we not here in danger of extreme subjectivism and arbitrary preferences?

Accepting of course the difficulties and the threatening dangers, I think, regrettably, that this is how the matter stands: namely, that only some formal elements (assuming that we possess a definition of this term) and only some content elements are aesthetically valuable. Moreover, this value is, it seems, in many cases relative, depending on the context in which the given element of the work appears. We must also allow for the third point of view—focusing on congruence—in discussing the aesthetic value of a musical work, but in this case too we cannot go to the extreme of postulating that only combinations of formal or of content elements may be aesthetically valuable and not any of those elements singly. A discussion in terms of an absolute either/or prejudges the case and cannot lead to a solution of the problem.

While it would be too early to attempt a solution of the problem here, I wish to point to some examples of aesthetically valuable qualities in order to save us from a one-sided solution and help us to agree that in a musical work these types of qualities do appear.

It seems that in a musical work the aesthetically valuable can be both the purely sound elements and those that constitute the nonsounding elements but appear in strict conjunction with musical constructs. Thus richness or fullness of tone in a violin composition, the sonorousness of tone in brass instruments, the hardly describable colorings of a piano's tones, the "velvet" quality of the flute's tone are aesthetically positive values, whereas thinness, weakness, or squeakiness of a violin, the roughness, sharpness, or loudness in the sound of various trumpets, the "glassiness" or shallowness of a piano's tone are aesthetically negative values. One might still argue whether such elements constitute the determinants only of a specific performance and not of the musical work. Undoubtedly these qualities are realized in performance, but they are also envisaged in the work. In principle, the composer selects such qualities of sounds as are aesthetically positively valuable. He therefore postulates the selection of suitable instruments and suitable performers capable of producing certain tonal qualities from their instruments (always assuming the instruments have the required capacity). But it is possible that the composer might select such sound-constructs as have qualities or tones of a negative aesthetic value but in combination with other qualities become positively valuable. We may say, therefore, that at least some of the above-mentioned determinations of tones constitute aesthetically valuable qualities and appear in the work itself. But there may also be tonal determinations that in themselves are aesthetically neither negative nor positive, that simply have a structural role in the work but are in themselves aesthetically indifferent.

The same may be said of complete sound-constructs. Some of them (whole melodies, for example) or their clusters have a positive aesthetic value, while others have a negative value, are simply ugly. Certain tempi and rhythms selected for sound-constructs have a positive aesthetic value, others a negative one. We say "that was played too fast," and therefore the singing quality of the melodic line "did not come over," or that certain selections of chords became blurred because they were not properly sustained. These comments apply both to the performance and to the work itself. Similarly the choice of *piano* for a specific sound-construct may have a positive aesthetic value, whereas the same sound-construct played *forte* acquires a negative value.

The various nonsounding elements of a work may be aesthetically valuable in a positive or negative way. An emotional quality like a repulsive feeling of misery is aesthetically negative or at least may conflict with a work's other emotional qualities. On the other hand, other qualities are "moving" and positively valuable. They include tragedy (which may permeate the coloring of the whole tonal harmony), suffering or mystery, sadness or sweetness (but not "sugariness," which is normally aesthetically negative), exultation, charm, happiness, eroticism (of certain melodies), excitement, or terror and fear followed by release of tension. Qualities such as eeriness, strangeness, and daemonism may be either positive or negative, depending on their intensity or the circumstances of their appearance. We must also remember that the simultaneous appearance or immediate succession of positive elements, or of positive elements followed by negative ones (in certain harmonies or disharmonies, either "clashes" in pure sound or, metaphorically speaking, emotional clashes) often leads to new harmonic phenomena of a higher order that are positively valuable.

It is only on the basis of these various and heterogeneous selections of aesthetically valuable qualities that nonsounding qualities constitute themselves *in concreto* during a given performance, qualities that provide a closer determination of the given work's value and simultaneously constitute that value. There is the specific charm of an Italian song that arises from a feeling of love and the quite different charm of a Ukrainian song tinged with pensiveness or longing. There is the "lightness," combined with superficiality, of certain violin pieces by Paganini or Kreisler; there is such a thing as perspicuity and "clarity" of the sound-constructs in Mozart's sonatas and the quite different perspicuity in the multivoiced structure of J. S. Bach's fugues, a perspicuity both in the individual voices and in their interrelationship along with a weight of sound-constructs and of superimposed emotional qualities. This is different from Mozart's works, which are often distinguished by a prettiness inconceivable in the serious beauty of Bach's music. In contrast with the perspicuity and simplicity of Bach's fugues, Wagner's *Ring* displays a tortuousness and complexity. There is the simplicity of the great classics and a certain *récherché* complicated richness of, say, Richard Strauss's symphonic poems. There is expansiveness in the melodies of Romantic music and Italian opera, contrasting with a certain angularity of Wagner's melodic structures, only occasionally broken by expansive love melodies such as Isolde's "Liebestod" in *Tristan* and some of Elsa's vocal lines in

Lohengrin. There is also an "eeriness" and a deliberate "barbarity" combined with a certain vulgarity or primitiveness in, say, Stravinsky's *Petrushka,* and the noble multicolored, multishaped architecture of the sound constructs full of metaphysical sheen and strangeness in his *Firebird.*

One could list indefinitely examples of such qualities that go beyond the pure sound of musical structures yet are most closely tied to various elements of aesthetically valuable sound-constructs and to their dependent nonsounding elements. It seems most strange that, as far as I know, no one has attempted so far even to list systematically (to say nothing of making a detailed analytical investigation of) these heterogeneous, aesthetically valuable qualities and the qualities of values. Only this would have enabled us to see which aesthetically valuable musical elements may, or even must, appear simultaneously and lead to an ultimate positively valuable sound-construct, as they either cannot appear simultaneously within the same work or, if they do, lead to an aesthetically negative cacophony. Finally, what are the ultimate, synthetic, total qualities of values that constitute themselves in the selection of these qualities and are not the fullness of the ultimate aesthetic value of the given work, that is, of the work as a whole and not of its specific fragments?[26] I am not of course attempting this analysis. All I have said is intended merely to show that the work itself displays *in concreto* what ought to be called its aesthetic value and that this value is something nonsounding, although its

26. We must remember that a musical work progresses in a time (in its own *time*) and only in the sequence of all its phases, the value of the individual fragments reveals itself, together with the organization of the totality and specific synthesis of the succeeding values forming themselves into the value of the totality. Here lie the special secrets of construction, not only in music but also in all temporally extended works of art, secrets that can only be revealed in analyses of individual works.

ultimate basis is not and cannot be anything but the sound-constructs appearing in the work with their varied formal and material properties.[27] And the whole musical work is, if I may so state it, designed to embody some such aesthetic value. This is the musical work's destiny or message as a work of art, irrespective of what further goals music may have in men's lives and in human culture generally. I have no intention either of denying or criticizing these possible secondary goals of musical works and of art works generally. I wish merely to state that they are secondary because their realization is possible only *through* an embodiment in a work of art perceived *in concreto,* that is, appearing in a particular performance of a specific aesthetic object in its manifest value. Without this there can be no art and no goal for art that is social, cultural, or otherwise.

27. Here lies the problem whose solution divides the "formalists," that is, those who regard only sound-constructs as elements of a musical work, from the "nonformalists" who additionally admit nonsounding elements. The problem is whether sound-constructs designate univocally and necessarily imply the appearance in the work of evident nonsounding elements, in particular of emotional qualities and qualities that are aesthetically valuable. While I cannot investigate this problem in detail, from what I have said so far, it will be clear that I am inclined to give an affirmative reply. But the problem is not so simple and the answer may be different, depending on the work's structure and especially on the type of sound-constructs appearing in a work. Here I was concerned only with deciding the fundamental issue of whether nonsounding elements can appear in a work at all.

6

How Does a Musical Work Exist?

Our discussion so far will enable us to consider the ontological status of a musical work.

Such a work originates in specific, creative, psychosomatic acts by the composer. These may culminate in the work's being notated in a musical score, as has been the practice for centuries, or in immediate performance by the composer, in which case we speak of improvization. Because of the imperfection of musical notation, the score is an incomplete, schematic prescription for performance. It fixes only certain aspects of its sound-base, whereas the remaining ones and especially the nonsounding elements, are only partially defined and within certain limits open to various interpretations. Both the fixed and the open elements have been conceived by the composer as fully defined and fixed, but he does not command a musical notation that would do them justice. Until recently we had no other ways of notating musical works except as schematic products. It is true that at least some of the undetermined features fixed in the musical notation flow indirectly from the elements of the work, but they can only be uniquely determined and fixed in the specific performances of the work. If, however, the work remains in the form in which it has been notated, these further elements remain existentially potential, as though there were only a possibility of their future realization in individual performances. Actually, in the work itself as notated, we have gaps or areas of indeterminateness which can be removed only in performance.[1] The fact that such gaps or areas of indeterminateness are found in a musical work is sufficient reason to regard the work designated by its score as a purely intentional object whose origins spring from the creative acts of the composer and whose ontic base rests directly in the score.[2]

Someone might object that we no longer must fix musical works by such imperfect means as musical notation. We may use gramophone records or tape-recordings, thus achieving a full definition of a musical work and collapsing the argument that the work is not a real but only an intentional object. The gramophone record would also insure that, at least in principle, we could have identically sounding works, a state of affairs that would affect crucially our discussion regarding the identity of a musical work.

Let us first of all observe that with regard to the musical work on a gramophone record made by the composer, we would in many cases obtain the work in a faulty performance, for composers are not generally good interpreters of their own works. And in many cases where more than one instrument is involved, especially in orchestral works, this would be quite impossible, even if the composer were a good conductor. Calling on the aid of good performers, say famous pianists, does not remove the danger of possible deviations from the original. The fact that gramophone records wear out and that gramophone equipment is not perfect

1. Something similar occurs in a theatrical performance that in its staging comprises the performance of a certain written work.

2. I have elsewhere shown in detail that a schematic construct with areas of indeterminateness is and must be a purely intentional object whose mode of existence is heteronymous and dependent on acts of consciousness. See my *The Literary Work of Art* and *Does the World Exist?*, volume 2.

leads to further possibilities of deviation from what the work ought to be. In any event, this is a record of a work in performance and not of the work itself. Surely what is recorded on wax or tape is not the work itself but certain effects arising from sound waves broadcast by the vibrant parts of the instrument upon which a given piece has been performed. And vice versa, the recorded traces of those sound waves played back on a suitable instrument give us a new performance of the work, which undoubtedly is very close to the first one, with properties affecting the realization of the new performance. The only part of the work which is now being realized (in the second performance) is a system of sound waves that, since they constitute a physical impulse for our hearing organ, make it possible for us to hear the performance. But what is directly conveyed to us in this way are only the sounds themselves, and these always with small deviations from the intentionally designated original, deviations that within certain limits may be of no consequence for aesthetic perception and for the subsequent constitution of the work in performance.

These sounds must be interpreted by the listener as the work's sound base. Only through the understanding of this base and through appropriate acts of consciousness do these sounds designate the artistically significant remainder of the musical work, beginning with sound-constructs and ending with the nonsounding elements of the work, in particular its aesthetically valuable qualities and the aesthetic value itself. Here the interpretation of the performance to some extent removes the "gaps" we have sensed in the musical work— though not all of them, as this is, on the whole, impossible— but they are replaced only with a system of certain qualities that in themselves are nothing more than concretions of qualities ideally belonging to the work. Thus, with the method of realizing or recording the work that we have just discussed, nothing in effect is realized but only concretized. The work itself remains like an ideal boundary at which the composer's intentional conjectures of creative acts and the listeners' acts of perception aim. The work thus seems to be an intentional equivalent of a higher order, belonging to a whole variety of intentional acts. These acts, of course, are formed by real people possessing real sense organs, who employ these organs either in the composition of musical work or in its realization in new performances or in listening to successive new performances. At that ideal boundary, the work remains one and the same in contrast to the many concretions in specific performances and thus, as I have already shown, it is in some respects de-individualized, although it does not cease to be an artistic individual in the sense previously defined. Whether this ideal boundary can ever be reached in individual performances and hearings or whether there must always be certain deviations and falsifications, which at times may be very acute, is a problem of the identity of a musical work. It is much more difficult to solve the problem here than in the case of a painting or work of architecture, since we do not have an "original" object as we do when an artist completes a painting or builds a specific edifice. In whatever way we might seek to solve this difficulty, which in the present case becomes so acute, the problem itself is the best proof that a musical work is not a real but a purely intentional object and, strictly speaking, one of a higher order.

Even if we were naive realists and believed that all sensible qualities of objects given in sensible perception constitute the real properties of physical objects and that, therefore, a grouping of sounds is something real, we would still not be able to regard the musical work as a real object. I have already shown that the musical work, as an artistic creation that because of its very nature ought to be perceived in an appropriately developing aesthetic experience, is not identical with the arrangement of concrete sounds heard in specific performances and constituting the performances' acoustic bases. As I have shown, the musical work does, in many of its artistically significant details, go outside the qualities of concrete sounds. Yet, it never attains the status of concrete sounds because these sounds are spatially and temporarily individuated objects, whereas a musical work is a supraindividual and supratemporal structure, its individuality being purely qualitative. These facts constitute the base of my second argument in favor of regarding a musical work as a purely intentional object with its original source in a specific real object and its ground of continued existence in a series of other real objects.

To ascribe the character of an intentional object to a musical work is not, however, synonymous with, or even equivalent to, recognizing it as a certain psychic reality or with turning it into something subjective. In my interpretation, a musical work remains something that we can create only intentionally and not in reality. We cannot endow it with the ontic autonomy that characterizes all real objects, including all psycho-physical subjects and their experiences. Had the musical work itself been a mental or a conscious experience, it would be just as real and existentially autonomous as all human experiences are, but it never is an experience or any part of it. If we were to treat it in this way, we would subjectivize it. This is avoided by the thesis that in accord with experience proclaims a musical work to be itself the product of certain conscious and psycho-physical acts of realization as well as being an object given to a subject listening to a given performance. This object, as purely intentional, is neither purely the perceptual experience in which it is given nor an experience that creatively designates the object nor yet any part or element of these experiences. It is solely something to which these experiences refer; it is neither mental nor subjective.

It was not my aim here to present a general theory of intentional objects. Others have done this before me. I have attempted elsewhere to make it more precise and correct it in certain respects.[3] The present study supplies only detailed material for this general theory, and I must, at this point, emphasize that the attempt to show that a musical work is a purely intentional object constitutes an element in my protracted struggle to collect as many varied arguments as possible against the idealistic conception of the real world as an intentional object of a particular type. This effort is not, as some say, an expression of my supposedly idealistic position. To avoid misunderstandings, which might arise from the ascription to me of statements I have never made, I must add a few remarks without, however, any detailed justification.

In accepting the proposition that no purely intentional object is real, I ipso facto logically accept the converse; namely, that no real object is purely intentional. I accept both these propositions not so much because of their logical relationship, but because I see a fundamental difference between the form and mode of existence of real and purely intentional objects. Because of the mode of existence of purely intentional objects, I also accept the proposition that the existence of purely intentional objects implies the existence of certain real objects. Specifically, with reference to musical works, we may agree that they exist heteronomously insofar as there are also existentially autonomous objects; specifically, real objects—namely, the composer and his mental and physical acts, which lead to the creation of the given musical work. Insofar as a musical work is to exist as an object that, al-

---

3. See *Does the World Exist?*, volume 2, chapter 10.

though purely intentional, is nevertheless intrasubjectively accessible (and therefore one and the same for various psycho-physical subjects—for the composer and his listeners), then there must additionally exist some method of preserving the work and making it accessible to a variety of subjects through the score or specific performances. The constitution of a musical work as an intersubjective aesthetic object demands that both the composer and the listeners should fulfill certain specific mental and physical acts called aesthetic experience or, if you wish, aesthetic perception. This perception in turn is possible only if certain real objects that we call psycho-physical subjects, namely, human beings, really exist.

I do appreciate that one might push realist views further and declare that musical works, too, should be treated as certain real objects, and in particular as certain clusters of conscious experiences occurring in the composer and his listeners. As we have noted at the beginning of these reflections, such identification of a musical work with certain conscious experiences does not form a tenable thesis. Specifically, it is equivalent to the rejection of the existence of, say, Beethoven's *Pathétique Sonata* and the recognition only of the existence of several collections of conscious experiences, none of which, incidentally, is the *Pathétique Sonata* or any of its performances. In such a case, there is no music and nothing for us to discuss. Naturally, anyone interested in the psychology of particular collections of experiences, or in the relevant area of sociology, will have a good deal of material to work on, but persisting in the position that there are no musical works, he will undoubtedly find great difficulties in establishing the scope and examining the properties of those collections of experiences he is seeking. But this is not my problem.

7

The Question of the Unity
of a Musical Work

As a conclusion to my investigations I wish to discuss two issues that are important to the philosophical notion of a musical work. The first concerns the question of its unity or wholeness, while the second is a matter of its identity, to which I have already referred, and the manner in which this identity can be demonstrated in the multiplicity of its specific performances and our perception of them.

The first question is: how does a work consisting of many musical products and many parts constitute nevertheless a single work that does not fall apart into many unrelated musical products, that forms a unified, meaningful whole? To be sure, not every musical work is truly unified. Not every work constitutes an artistically meaningful whole. There are, however, works that are "bad" music, and they are bad partly because they disintegrate into unrelated acoustic products, even though they form an uninterrupted sequence in time. Yet, these actually unrelated parts are supposed—according to the intentions of the composer and the destination of the work of art which is to arise upon them—to belong to each other and form a unified whole. This in fact is the concept of art in general. The temporal sequence of these parts is not, however, sufficient to constitute them into a single work and a unified, meaningful, artistic whole, for there is something lacking in the qualitative determination and structure that prevents the achievement of unity and wholeness in the given work. It is an amalgam, but not a single work. And the problem is precisely whether there can exist some attribute and form of the parts (the specific, musical products constituting the work) such that, despite their variety, despite the gaps that at times appear among them, despite the fact that in performance one of them already disappears from the field of perception while another one emerges, they all together make up a meaningful whole.

First, with regard to the "parts" of a musical work: they are of different types. There are the "big" parts, such as the four movements of a classical sonata or symphony. These, as we have already noted, are actually separated by intervals. For instance the Allegro comes to an end; then for a while nothing is played (for how long depends on the work, but sometimes also on the sensitivity of the performer or conductor) and then the Adagio or the Andante begins. There is no music between these two parts. Are there four separate works performed at short intervals, or is there a single work with four parts? Is this perhaps a matter of convention or habit so that we could treat them either as one work or as four?

Within each of those big parts there are smaller and even very small ones, ultimately particular phrases and even, as one might say, individual sounds and specific clusters of simultaneously sounding tones. It might be asked: is not how we determine these small parts again a matter of convention or habit? Do we treat each one of them as a separate whole or do we take them all together as a single work? And if a musical work is indeed a purely intentional object, is not the conventionalist approach the most appropriate—would it not enable us without difficulty to solve the present problem? Any such naive interpretation of my thesis about the pure intentionality of musical works and works of art in general would be wrong. We can listen to and interpret a musical work in any way we like, but it does not follow that we shall always be faithful to it (that is, that we shall accurately reflect its properties and its specific nature) and that we shall always be dealing with a work of art and with just this work of art that is the given musical work. For the fact that the work is an intentional object does not at all mean that, once it has been created, it does not contain links among its elements and moments and its own orderliness that constitute its individuality and specific character. On the contrary—as every creative performer will testify—in the realm of every proper work of musical art there are very close links among its parts, and this linking often presents considerable difficulties to the performer. Thus, we should not immediately fall into the simplistic conventionalism that is so attractive to those who proclaim a comfortable skepticism as the highest wisdom.

Let us note that those "small" parts of a musical work— parts in a musical sense, and not in the sense of an arbitrary mental division of the temporal continuum into infinity— are very different and of different orders. They cannot be identified, as one might suppose, with specific moments of time in a given musical work. As I have tried to show above, there is indeed a certain link between the moments of time immanent in the given work and the musical products. Thus, these moments do contribute to the formation of the organization of musical time and also to the constitution of specific moments in the sphere of a given work. But, first, they are not that moment—assuming they can be fitted into it—but its musical fulfillment; and second, it is possible for them to stretch over the whole multiplicity of succeeding moments in a musical work. Yet, it is also possible that within a single moment one can detect a certain diversity of the parts of the musical work. One phrase may be so constructed that, covering only a single moment, it nevertheless contains elements of which it is constructed, even though these elements may consist in a single sound.

Such elements of a single phrase are probably the smallest kind of musical element of a musical work, which only exist in the boundaries of that sphere as elements of the work and for themselves. If these elements could be somehow isolated with the help of artificial instruments and in this isolation somehow perceived, they would not thus constitute an element of musical meaning and therefore of a musical part of the work. This smallest unit of meaning is at least the musical phrase, constructed as a whole from various strictly interrelated sounds, be they the inception of a certain melody or that of a single chord. Such a chord constitutes a musical unit, to a large extent independently of whether its duration is brief or it is sustained for a comparatively long time during which other musical units are contained simultaneously. The division of a musical work into smaller or larger parts does not in principle depend on a strictly temporal division into specific musical moments in which, during the performance of the work, they happen to be fully actualized. Rather, they depend on the structure or, if you will, the form of the auditory products that are part of the work, which differ from one another more or less clearly, and—with regard to the larger parts of a musical work—differ from one another in the relationships that exist between smaller parts and ultimately between the phrases.

A musical phrase may consist of a single sound, possibly repeated, but normally it is built up from a multiplicity of sounds that constitute its members. If, nevertheless, it is, or is supposed to be, a single phrase, despite the multiplicity of its members, there must be something imposing a unity on this multiplicity, which insures that it does not fall apart into a scattered multiplicity of unrelated sounds but rather structures itself upon them into an indivisible whole. This can be nothing else but a sounding aspect (gestalt) and special in this respect: that it may extend beyond the boundaries of a single musical "now" and therefore spread itself only in musical time. This does not of course exclude the possibility that it may sometimes be accommodated within a single musical "now." If, then, the phrase is to be heard—and only then will it be present to the listener as a totality that constitutes an element of the musical work—this will be on the condition that the listener's perception reach into the closest past and bind it into a single whole with the actual present. This reaching into the past is rather a holding of the just-vanished past in a certain actuality so that it should remain present, although it is already passed or passing.

In his *Phenomenology of Internal Time-Consciousness,* Husserl called this "holding" of just-past actuality "retention." In the case of musical phrases or products constructed from a series of phrases and extending over a long period of musical time, whose sounding aspect covers several moments and realizes itself in them, one requires in perception not only retention but additionally a certain specific palpable expectation of that which is about to occur, which Husserl correlatively called "protention." I had earlier called attention to the fact that in musical works there often occurs "an announcement" of what is to follow through that which, at that instant of the present, constitutes the fulfillment of the moments of musical time. This announcement constitutes an objective correlative of the developing auditory aspects with palpable expectation, that is, a protention. This correlative occurs subjectively with the addition of retention and protention to actual perception and objectively with the spread of a single auditory aspect over the whole sequence of instants of musical time. Thus, there comes about within the bounds of a musical work a construction of larger musical parts that—within the confines of what a sole auditory aspect binds together, for instance a single melody—constitute tightly knit and uniform totalities.[1]

But we cannot assert that every musical work as a whole contains only a single auditory aspect and therefore only a single sound product. This certainly is not the case, with the possible exception of very small works, for instance, certain primitive folk songs. Artistic music usually consists in works that contain many sound products with various auditory aspects. The variety introduces a certain richness into the structure of a musical work and may constitute one of its values. This of course complicates the issue of the unity of a musical work, since it cannot be the case that all the sound products appearing in the work should be bound with a single auditory aspect. Although we cannot ignore the fact that sometimes two consecutive auditory aspects lead to the emergence of a new higher-order aspect, which includes the other two, there surely is no larger work in which all the musical products ultimately lead to a single auditory aspect covering the whole of the work. In consequence, various

1. In order to grasp such a totality it is not enough to possess retention and protention as a surround of the actualizing perception (more accurately: here the perception of auditory aspects includes retention and protention related strictly to a direct grasp of what is sounding "now"). For we cannot exclude a certain kind of deafness to auditory aspects: the listener hears specific notes, even perhaps whole phrases, but does not hear the aspect that embraces in itself, as a specific simple quality, a multiplicity of sounds stretching over several instants. Such people, deaf to auditory aspects, do not qualify strictly speaking as music listeners, but neither do they qualify as musical theorists, because that which precisely constitutes the specificity of a musical work remains beyond their experience. They hear scattered multiplicities of sounds, they do not hear music. I cannot persuade such people that I am right in my whole conception of a musical work. Nor will such people be led to the perception of a musical work through "associations" created through repetitions, as Zofia Lissa insists.

possible answers suggest themselves to the question of the bases of the unity of the musical work.

It may be that each of these parts corresponds to a different type of musical work, in view of the way in which the parts of the work create its totality. But it may also be the case that the specific sound products of a given work relate to each other only because they succeed one another, or belong to one another in a certain characteristic manner, or finally because they bring about the appearance of one new element that unites all the sound products together. In the first instance, the work basically lacks unity and its totality depends only on the temporal contiguity of the sound products it contains; it is an amalgam more or less devoid of artistic meaning. In an extreme case, where, for instance, the particular phases of the work not only are not related to each other but are clearly in opposition, leading to a product of cacophony (as, for instance, if one attempted to construct a work made up of the first bars of all Chopin's preludes), this sequence of phases would not persuade us to accept the unity of this work—to agree that we are dealing with a single work. There may be much less glaring instances of a discrepant work, having a true amalgam of unrelated sound products, in which, nevertheless, there are certain signs that we should treat the given work as one, albeit one that is an artistic failure. For we surely have elements that unify the tonal products, such as the maintenance of the same key (not an essential condition of the unity of a musical work) or the maintenance of the same rhythm or measure in all the musical products appearing in the given work. What is lacking is artistic invention, so that a particular part of the work may (without loss but also without profit for the totality of the work) be replaced by another part appearing sooner or later.

But what is the situation when musical products appearing within one work not only follow one another but also belong to one another? Various bases of their belonging to one another are possible. First, two chronologically contiguous sound products may dovetail into each other as a result of the phenomenon I have already described, whereby one sound product passes into the other or where the second one alludes to the first. These transitions may be quite varied, and it is the task of detailed investigations of the composition of musical works to analyze them more closely. An additional basis for musical products relating to one another—apart from the supportive maintenance of the same rhythm, measure, tempo, or key—is the resultant harmony or even disharmony between two successive tonal products. The aspect qualities of these products somehow serve one another as complements or contrasts. The second product constitutes a special kind of completion of the first but is, so to speak, a qualitative completion. Their harmony or disharmony is also a qualitative element, although it cannot be regarded as simply a sounding aspect. As such, it is of course nonsounding, although sounding products form its basis. This harmony or disharmony is a very special feature in that it appears only after the appearance of the second sounding product; that is, at the moment when the first already belongs to the past, both in terms of the work itself and in terms of its performance and, moreover, at the moment when that second product is already developed so that its sounding aspect has revealed itself to the listener. One can paradoxically assert that this qualitative harmony of the two sounding products is not manifest while listening to the work until both products have already been performed and are no longer present in musical experience. The perception of a musical work, however, does not consist in a simple hearing of constantly new sounds. It is much more complicated, demanding not only auditory retention and protention, but also grasping of the after-sounds of already heard phases of the work. It requires a "living memory," through which the phases that have passed but are not too distant from the current phase, are present as reminiscences, at least in their final synthetic sounding.[2] Their reminiscent present constitutes the phenomenal base for the constitution of the phenomenon of harmony between two associated sound products.

Finally, the third way in which two successive sound products may belong to each other arises from the same emotional quality that characterizes both these products. Despite the existence of different auditory aspects, when listening to them we find ourselves in the same emotional atmosphere. In other words, a unity of atmosphere constitutes one of the bases for the different tonal products to belong to each other and, therefore, one of the bases of the unity of a musical work. It is obvious that with regard to musical products of one and the same work, their association may occur simultaneously on all the different bases I have distinguished. Consequently the unity of the work is strengthened. Naturally, the types of meaningfulness of the artistic totality of the work may be extremely various, depending above all on what tonal products appear in the work and what constitutes the basis for their association. But this is a matter for detailed study of the structure of musical works—a very difficult study that so far has been undertaken only to a minimal extent. We have, however, to content ourselves with merely pointing to the principle of coherence and artistic unity of a musical work, and I have no illusions that I have exhausted all the possibilities of the formation of a musical work as a whole.

There is, however, one problem requiring discussion, regarding the unity of works consisting of large parts or

2. I have discussed "live memory" in my *Cognition of a Literary Work.*

movements such as exist in a sonata or a symphony. In those cases, as we have already noted, there are gaps between specific parts, wholly unoccupied by any musical products. What is more, these gaps do not even belong to the temporal cluster of the work. They are different from the pauses that often appear within the bounds of these large sections, which are measured in relation to the given work, so that all continuity in the development of the work is here broken. Were we to treat the musical work, at least in performance, as a certain process developing in time, then—in accordance with general assertions regarding the identity of processes that I am unable to develop here[3]—one would have to agree that these gaps bring about the disintegration of such forms as the classical sonata into four separate works that at best constitute a certain cycle.[4] But it seems that a true musical work develops in performance into a certain product that in its temporal spread is reminiscent of the structure of a process but differs from a simple process precisely because it is an organized totality in which specific parts belong to each other. In the case of the best possible composition, they postulate each other or they fulfill the postulates of other parts constituting their fulfillment or completion. This circumstance will, I think, enable us to categorize as a single work

3. See my *Does the World Exist?*, volume 2, section 62.

4. Chomiński has lately proposed the thesis that Chopin's twenty-four preludes form a single unity. I have indeed heard performances during which all the twenty-four preludes were played, though for instance Ashkenazy played them without a break, while Kedra played the last twelve after an interval. I do not think this case parallels that of a sonata or a symphony: Chopin's preludes do not form a single work but a cycle of works, so that they can be performed together; but in principle we do not gain a great deal by playing them all one after another, nor do we lose a great deal when they are played separately. I do not think that we could, for example, demonstrate that Prelude No. 5 is a continuation of Prelude No. 4.

the four movements of a sonata so composed despite the breaks between parts.

If these breaks are not to upset the artistic unity of the work, they cannot be too long (lasting, say, hours or days) or too short; nor would it contribute to the maintenance of artistic values in the work if we were to remove the breaks altogether and play the whole sonata "at one go," assuming that such continuity is not in fact indicated in the score (which cannot be ruled out). Let us examine this matter through an example.

The removal of breaks is impossible in all those cases where the succeeding movements are composed in different keys and also possibly with a different beat. Both types of change do sometimes occur without affecting the unity of the sonata as an artistic product. If we did not have a break between the two parts, there would occur at the juncture of the two parts a clear jolt, which would be sensed by the listener as a fault in the work. Further, the closing bars of a preceding movement often have the very special character of a conclusion, demanding at least a moment's silence, without which the closure would appear artistically nonsensical. The opening of the next movement is not so clearly demarcated, especially if we consider that it has been preceded by a closure, but even so this opening insists that it is not the continuation of a previous movement. Thus, on account of their structure, the two adjacent movements postulate a break.

There are deeper reasons that justify the need for breaks. In order to perceive adequately the Adagio cantabile in Beethoven's *Pathétique Sonata,* we require the after-sound or at least the general impression of pathos and vitality of the sonata's preceding movement. Silence, because it introduces peace and calm, constitutes here an aesthetically significant contrast to that vitality, allowing its after-sound to dissipate and allowing the listener to prepare himself for the totally different kind of emotion in the succeeding Adagio cantabile. The melancholy lyricism of the Adagio represents a descent through several layers into the depth of emotion, a descent not possible without a struggle, were it not preceded by both the pathos and the vitality of the preceding movement and their gradual dissipation, so that we are still under the impression of the first part but, in a supervening calm, are becoming ready to receive a new phase of the work with a different general atmosphere.

So much for the need and the function of a break at this point in the sonata. But the Adagio cantabile also represents the unveiling of a different side—another sphere of emotion concealed behind the majestic pathos of the Grave, intertwined with the rousing vitality of the Allegro molto—an unveiling that in a specific way illumines that pathos and reveals its externality. Were these movements of the *Pathétique Sonata* divided by an hour's break and the listener's time filled with mundane jobs, erasing from his mind the impressions of the first movement, both movements would reveal themselves shorn of all those secondary yet no less essential, palpable characteristics flowing from the contrast between the two movements—a contrast that may be apprehended directly whenever the Adagio follows the Grave and the Allegro molto after a short break but vanishes completely after a break that is too long. An adequate perception of the Adagio does not depend solely on hearing and understanding just the tonal products which appear in it, but also on grasping in their fullness the concrete emotional qualities, which manifest themselves over the cluster of these products only when the Adagio is perceived in the aura of the atmosphere conjured up by the first movement. Still, it is necessary that the atmosphere of the Grave and the Allegro molto should by now be only an aura or an after-sound, to allow the listener to switch emotionally and perceptually and enable him to emerge from the total power of the pathos and violent action of the preceding Adagio. He should then be able to synthesize his aesthetically significant impressions and to receive a new aspect of musical and emotional harmony without completely leaving the emotional aura of the preceding pathos.

This is the way I see the function of the break between the relevant movements of the *Pathétique Sonata*. Naturally, the function of such breaks is different in different works, and we would have to examine their roles individually in specific music. What is crucial, however, is that the break as such—even though it does not belong to the temporal continuum of the work and although it is an absence of auditory products—nevertheless enters into the totality of the work, performing an important constructional role as it unveils for the listener the proper face of the work. Apparently it divides, but it does so in such a way that in the end it reveals the relationship between the movements it divides. The break must, however, remain empty; it must not be filled with applause or the eating of sweets.

Assuming, of course, that the movements are properly constructed, breaks between such movements are essential to the work and cannot either be removed or extended without creating changes unfavorable to the artistic unity. Although the break is an absence of sound products, it basically constitutes an element of the work and is far from threatening or demolishing unity. Breaks are designated (perhaps at times approximately) by the work's movements, and it turns out that they are not so much an absence as a certain positive element of the musical work. It is implied, of course, that the adjacent movements are in themselves so constructed and contain such qualities that they belong to one another in the sense discussed above, for otherwise the break cannot perform the functions just described.

So far, of course, this is a purely formal solution that needs to be supplemented with an analysis of particular works, showing concrete relationships between the auditory products appearing in the work and their elements. All I have been able to do here is to demonstrate the possibility of grounding the artistic unity of musical works consisting of several large sections, without showing the effective unity of specific works, say, the symphonies of Beethoven. Our claim to having shown the way towards solving the question of the unity of a musical work may perhaps become more persuasive if we compare those works in which there does exist a relationship between the movements of the work, grounded in the properties of its auditory products, to those in which there is no such relationship. To make the contrast vivid we may imagine such a work that lacks artistic unity. Let us imagine that an orchestra performs a symphony consisting of the following movements: it starts with the first movement of Beethoven's Fifth Symphony, then—after the customary short break between movements—it performs a symphonic poem by Debussy, followed by a toccata by J. S. Bach, concluding with an orchestral transcription of an aria from Act III of Puccini's *Madame Butterfly*. The total absence of any connection between the putative movements of this kind of "symphony," the glaring incompatability of styles, of atmosphere, of texture and so on, are so profound that surely no one would acknowledge the artistic unity of this amalgam of differing products. In contrast, the artistic unity of, for example, Beethoven's Fifth Symphony would become manifest. But the fact that we do know such unities from experience—although it may be argued whether such totalities are in principle possible—does not of course mean that the bases of the unity of a work that I have here indicated are in fact capable of performing this role. The reader must take up the critical consideration of this matter, and I would be grateful for his help in this difficult but crucial investigation.

8

The Problem of the Identity of a Musical Work in Historical Time

Let us finally turn to the question of the identity of a musical work during a specified period in our historical time. This problem arises especially in longer periods that include a succession of different styles and even perhaps of fundamental ideals concerning musical and artistic aspirations. Old works live, that is, they are played and heard, in new musical epochs and while they are differently interpreted, they are, nevertheless, regarded as being the same as they were in the past, although they used to be played in different ways. In order to appreciate fully the difficulties arising when we wish to confirm our conviction regarding the identity of musical works that sometimes stay alive over a number of centuries, we first have to bring the problem into sharper focus. In the existing formulations of the problem of a musical work's identity, the term "musical work" remains ambiguous. Second, the formulation of the problem suggests two approaches that need to be clearly distinguished: a purely ontological or ontic formulation of the problem and an epistemological or an aesthetic formulation. Finally, we need to stress that the question can be variously formulated, depending upon the method of "fixing" a musical work.

Let us start with the last issue: the problem varies depending on whether in a particular case notation is the only way of preserving that work, or whether there are other, better, ways of preserving it: that is, through gramophone records and tapes. I have already indicated that musical notation enables us to preserve only some features of a musical work, designating a schematic product that may never be played or sung in this form but must, in performance, be completed to the fullness of a concrete product, in principle as complete as it has been composed—or at least is to be composed—in the composer's creative acts.[1] Given this method of registering a musical work, we have to distinguish between (a) the musical work as an artistic product taken in exactly the way it is intentionally determined by the musical score; (b) the musical work as an ideal aesthetic object; and (c) the musical work as a concrete aesthetic product.[2]

In the first instance we have a schematic product, but it is salutary to remind ourselves what, in such circumstances, is fully determined in it and where there are areas of indeterminacy. Musical notation directly fixes certain sounds, their duration and co-presence or sequence, their approximately determined absolute and relative pitch, their intensity, and

1. I add this caveat because it is problematic whether a composer is capable of concretizing the work in his creative imagination to such an extent that its concretion is fully determinate. It appears highly probable that even a composer endowed with a rich creative imagination imagines his work, before writing it down, only in a very schematic, impoverished, and telescoped form and that—as we know from the history of music—he supplements his acts of the imagination with effective performance, at least with regard to the crucial fragments (particularly in the case of grand orchestral works) but that he does not hear the work in all its fullness until the actual concert performance. Thus, in many instances, it is only the performance that enables him to judge whether or not he had composed a successful piece. We can say however, that the composer aims in principle at obtaining in imagination the full work and thinks about it as univocally determined in all detail, although when he comes to notate it he must ignore the various details, fully determined as they are in his mind, because he lacks a means of registering them.

2. "Ideal" is of course an ambiguous term and may refer to the mode of existence of the objects of mathematical inquiry, but it also may indicate a state of perfection. I am here using the term in the second sense, and its application will soon become clear.

their coloring. Sometimes we find in the score such performance instructions as *legato* or *staccato* or a slur sign to indicate that a number of notes are to be played as a unit. Finally, we often find in the score such verbal instructions as "gaily," "seriously," "with feeling," and so on, all of these being general instructions giving rough indications of the class of emotional qualities that by means of a particular playing technique, are to appear in the performance of the work. Already, in these various elements of a musical work fixed with the aid of notes, we come across a variety of imprecisions and blurrings, possible only in purely intentional objects, which in specific performance are necessarily removed and replaced with sharp, univocal determinations. The choice of these univocal determinations is of course related to the talent and artistic sensibility of the performer.

In the case of a musical work fixed through a score, all the rest of it remains undetermined and these areas of indeterminacy have to be removed in performance by the performer in ways he judges appropriate or in which he just happens to succeed. These indeterminate areas of the work do not depend only on the various nonsounding elements that stem from its sounding properties (especially its tonal properties) but also from the various elements of the sound base. For example, the score does not on the whole determine which sounds in the whole sound mass have to be distinguished or accentuated to enable, for example, the melodic line to stand out from its sound background or to bring out a characteristic element of the form of the musical product or finally to allow a certain emotional quality to make its appearance. Nor on the whole do we see defined a quality of "touch" (say, on a piano) or the method of "extracting" a certain timbre (for instance, on the violin) to achieve a specific fullness or softness of sound or, on the other hand, a certain "hardness" indicated in a particular work or its phase. Even if at times we find the appropriate descriptions in a score, these are usually only vague verbal descriptions, impossible to replace with a precise meaning and causing the "blurrings" I have referred to. Particularly in orchestral works whose performance entails many people playing a variety of instruments, several characteristics of the work remain indeterminate in the score—above all, the "profile" of specific sound products that in the sound mass are supposed either to stand out or be merged—so that both the conductor and members of the orchestra have to select one among many possibilities. The indeterminancies include those that are purely technical and that the composer can neither foresee nor precisely formulate. Thus, for instance, those elements of tonal coloring that depend upon the technical mastery of the instrument—to say nothing of those dependent upon the psychosomatic state of the performers during performance—cannot be indicated either in the score or in words. If, for example, we take into account how both piano construction and playing techniques have changed in the past hundred years, it becomes clear that Chopin could not have foreseen how his works performed on today's instruments would sound. He naturally "heard" them within those qualities of sound coloring in which he performed them himself, qualities then possible in the prevailing state of piano manufacture. But even this coloring he had no way of indicating in his scores, nor can we be sure whether he would regard the present-day sound of his works as appropriate. Thus, these specific colorings of sounds and their clusters do not belong to the work itself as a schematic product, intentionally designated by the score, but rather as an aesthetic object, be it concrete or ideal.

As long as the score remains unchanged, the work as a schema will remain unchanged for centuries. Therefore, the identity of a work understood in this sense is not in question and does not raise special problems. But, as I have indicated, it is impossible to perform the schema on its own without additions and without making precise all those elements of the work that either do not appear in the schema or are indicated in it imprecisely. We cannot, therefore, hear the work in this schematic shape, and we cannot even imagine it in this way. For even though the auditory imagination, stimulated by, for example, a reading of the score, may complete the work's schema in many respects, the "profile" of the work that it provides will in many respects be blurred and incomplete. Anyone who is a good musician and a competent score reader may know what the work is to be like in respect to details unspecified in the score, but he will never be able to imagine it with respect to all its qualities that lie outside the schema.

But the identity of the work's schema is not enough to remove doubts regarding the identity of the musical work at different historical times. These doubts arise from the fact that in performance the variables are those that are not determined within the schema. Of course a specific performance may include variants with regard to those elements of the work determined by the score. Then we say that the given performance is faulty, or at any rate does not recreate the work it was intended to recreate.[3] But a performer who adheres to all the details fixed in the score may introduce such crucial changes with regard to remaining elements that we may indeed wonder whether this is still the same work. This is because those elements not fixed in the schema are precisely the details that belong to its profile as an aesthetic ob-

3. I include this possibility since, after all, it is possible for a performer consciously and deliberately to alter certain details of the work without lowering its value. He may even create something more perfect than the original work, but this no longer is an exact performance of a work notated in the score but of another work, albeit very similar to the original.

ject. What remains indeterminate are various aspects of the sound basis itself (for instance the timbre of the piano or violin sound, the greater or lesser clarity of the profile of specific sound structures, the proper or improper accentuation of specific sounds—be it in the development of the melody or the chord harmony—or inability to sustain the right tempo) on which depends the appearance or nonappearance of particular emotional qualities and aesthetically valuable qualities. In the first instance we shall have revealed all the work's beauties, while in the latter case it will be shorn of its values and will appear dead, boring, and long-winded. Someone might say, all this is true but what does it mean? Is it not simply that certain performances of the work are faulty? Does it really mean that the work itself changes in a crucial way to such an extent that it ceases to be itself? The answer is that in the given performances the work does not reveal itself in all its qualities, while in other performances its proper aesthetic character is better expressed.

Let us stress that whoever argues in this manner understands the work of music to be something other than the schema fixed by the score, irrespective of whether he is right or wrong regarding the issue of the work's identity. He has in mind a fully qualified aesthetic object, that is, one endowed with all the categories of elements we have already discussed, so that it is the most perfect musical product that we can possibly imagine arising out of the schema and that, in the fullness of its aesthetic value, may reveal itself in the best performance to a listener engaged in an adequate aesthetic perception of the given work in the given performance. In other words, he has in mind, when talking of a musical work, what I have described above as "an ideal aesthetic object." Understanding that it is possible and necessary for the listener to acquire this kind of general understanding of a musical work, the question arises whether in relation to an individual instance (say, Chopin's B Minor Sonata) it is possible to define univocally all the details of a musical work so understood. For only in an actual performance can we, in the fullness of musical experience, perceive the work's qualities. Do we have a "perfect" performance at our disposal? Is such a work (as it reveals itself to us in particular performances—assuming we have succeeded in achieving an adequate perception of the work) that "ideal aesthetic object" envisaged by the composer or his score?

Our initial response would be to deny the possibility of an ideal performance. But if we reflect a moment, we have to admit that we have no right to assert this, for we have no way of knowing whether in fact a particular performance does not represent accurately that profile of the work that it has to possess as an ideal aesthetic object. Practically speaking, we have no idea which of the performances we ought to accept as ideal. And we do not know this because, strictly speaking, we never come to know a musical work as an ideal aesthetic object. From the score, from the available performances, which in the end are never adequate in number, or from the composer's reports (and always assuming that these perceptions of the work are adequate) we can only speculate—on the whole much less adequately than the composer himself—what, in the given instance, that ideal aesthetic object ought to be. We can, however, by making a comparison with the work's score, exclude a certain range of performances that appear to us faulty. With regard to the remainder we do not, strictly speaking, know which of them come close to the work as an ideal aesthetic object or which, to some degree and in some manner, diverge from it.

We must take account of yet another factor about which we learn from the history of music, namely, that in particular epochs musical works are normally performed in a specific manner imposed by outstanding, highly individualistic performers and also dependent upon the general aesthetic taste of the epoch. Thus, within my own lifetime the method of performing piano works, and in particular the works of Chopin, seems to have undergone radical change. When I was young, in the period of neoromanticism, Chopin was performed in a decidedly emotional manner with an object of creating an atmosphere of gloom and despair.[4] These early performances exaggerated the intensity of emotional qualities at the expense of virtuoso elements, while today's performances of Chopin reveal to a much greater extent the great richness of purely tonal products and the brilliance of their forms. Whether or not I am accurate in the description of these changes, I assume my readers will acknowledge that at different times the same works by Chopin have been played in different ways. I have said "the same" works, but if we were to judge the contents of these works solely on the basis of performances taking place in different epochs, we

4. At that time, a legend gained currency regarding the way in which Przybyszewski played Chopin. He appears to have charmed his audiences with atmospheric playing, since technically, as we know today, his playing was inadequate. When I speak of that kind of interpretation I do not have Przybyszewski in mind, since I never heard him. But if we were to take Paderewski or Sliwinski and their contemporaries and if we were to compare their playing with Rubinstein's or Cortot's, the differences in interpretation are striking. In the light of the new style, the old form of interpretation will appear to us not only too emotional but positively sentimental. In any case, the purely tonal aspects of Chopin's works is now more prominent in all its artistic splendor, even though it might appear that as a consequence Chopin's music has, to some extent, been "deromanticized." Although the earlier style was probably closer to Chopin's own playing, a new aspect of his music, one which we had not previously felt, stands revealed in contemporary interpretations. This change probably came about not only because new performers have appeared but also because new compositions have realized not only fresh pianistic possibilities, but also a different sensibility, a certain emotional coolness foreign to Chopin.

would have to conclude that, for instance, the performances of Chopin's mazurkas by Paderewski designate an ideal aesthetic object that in many respects differs from the ideal designated by the same mazurkas as played by Szpinalski—as though the mazurkas themselves were in the course of time undergoing a slow transformation. What will the future bring? What will the new pianist be like? How different will be the listeners' attitudes and their tastes? Will not the interpretation of Chopin's works by future virtuosos—who will also be acquainted with new music that we cannot even perhaps intuit—depart even further from the manner in which Chopin himself realized his own works? How are we to settle the question as to whether these interpretations will be better or worse? Are we to follow the judgment of those who are more rigid in their response to music and recognize only the style of playing specific to the works' own epoch? They assume this attitude because they are not flexible enough to empathize with the work's constantly changing aspects that often relegate values previously actualized, but nevertheless seem compatible with values that are fully in accord with the tonal basis of the performed works. Or are we rather to accept various modes of interpreting Chopin's works in different epochs, claiming that only the aspect of the works manifest in contemporary performances is proper and uniquely consonant with the "original"?

How are we to settle this question, given that, strictly speaking, we are not acquainted with that original? And we are unacquainted with it not only because we were born after Chopin's death and have not heard him play even on records, but also because, if we were able to hear Chopin himself play, we would have no guarantee that he performed his own works well or that he interpreted them in the only possible manner, even assuming that, technically speaking, he was equal to the task.

The situation here is completely different from that in painting, for instance, where there exists an original in the sense of a pigmentation created by the artist, which constitutes an immediate ontic base for the work and determines its essential properties. In music we have only the score, which does not constitute any of the work's elements, or the authorial original performance. The work itself, designated through creative acts and fixed as regards some of its details in the score, is a product that extends so far beyond the authorial performances that it constitutes in relation to them a certain ideal that need not be realized in them. Once the creative process is at an end, this ideal is available to us only indirectly through notation or performances that embody it to a certain extent but without guarantee that they faithfully retain all details. There is no necessary direct connection between the work and its performances. Nor can the models be imitated directly, because they are either an incomplete set of performing instructions provided in the score of a particular aspect that the work acquires in someone else's performance (including the author's), an aspect perhaps falsified or one-sided and not exhausting the possibilities of the work.

Thus, we have many realizations of the same work in many performances including those by the composer. Assuming a purely aesthetic point of view; that is, one that takes into account the aesthetic value of a work above all else, a value that reveals itself in a particular performance, we could accept the manner in which we presume Chopin performed his works as the only acceptable one if we had proof that every other interpretation of his works not only detracted from the aesthetic value made possible by the musical products appearing in them, but moreover did not replace them with other values, so that in the end they became aesthetically impoverished. Experience, however, usually teaches us the opposite. A new style of performance admittedly removes certain aesthetic values present in the old interpretations, but it embodies new values that not only are in accord with the sound basis of the work but also accentuate more emphatically its specific values. From the purely aesthetic point of view we cannot exclude either the profile of Chopin's works that has emerged in previous epochs or that which reveals itself in performances of our own day.

Someone might reply: this is all very well, but Chopin's works are crucially connected with his creative personality. Therefore, only the profile that he has stamped upon his works is the proper one, especially since, by a happy coincidence, he was a masterly performer. All subsequent performances are deviations from the originals caused by the changed circumstances in which Chopin's works have since been performed. His own performances embody that ideal aesthetic object, that is, a perfect realization of the works. On the other hand, all later performances reveal "concrete aesthetic objects," all of which may be made available to listeners through the same score, but all differing more or less from the original so that it is quite sufficient for us not to regard them as the original. Only that original remains one and the same, but at the same time is not attainable in any other performance or in any new experiencing of aesthetic perception. If it seems to us today that we are hearing a Chopin mazurka in a particular performance, we are in essence victims of an illusion caused by the similarity existing between the original and the perceived, concrete, aesthetic object—the specific mazurka in a specific performance.

In adopting this historical approach we make certain assumptions that do not fit the facts. We talk as if Chopin played each of his compositions only once and in each case did so perfectly; that is, realizing to the full the aesthetic values of the works in accordance with his artistic intentions. In fact, he must have played them many times, not in the same way in every instance and not in every instance in the best way. Thus, his own performances, in the case of each of his works, did not designate an "original," that is, a unique "ideal aesthetic object" intended or realized by the composer, but rather defined a succession of such objects, each somewhat different with respect to such details as affected their aesthetic value. If we were to construct the supposed "original" of a particular work on the basis of its performances, we would have to choose either on the basis of a statistical average—which with reference to works of art would be a pointless procedure—or of a single performance that we would no longer treat from a historical point of view (since not only the chosen performance but all its performances are authorial performances) but from an aesthetic point of view with regard to that which is "the best." But "the best" is not supposed to mean that containing the highest aesthetic value, but that which is "the most faithful." How are we to decide this, since our acquaintance with the work is never direct but always mediated by a performance?

Second—and here is a special problem—it may appear that the "original" authorial performances do not contain any one that is "the best." When we have perceived and analyzed them, we may reach the conclusion that, for example, two performances are equally good but differ one from the other in quite significant ways. This is the astonishing fact: we may perform the same work (same according to the score) in different ways, with the different performances transmitting a work with different aesthetic values that, so it would appear, are equally high. Which of these did the composer intend to realize? Both? Just one of them, or perhaps some other performance with a lower aesthetic value, as though he himself was not sure what aesthetic values his work should and could embody? How can *we* pronounce upon this even if we had a number of such performances on record?

Undoubtedly we can be greatly helped by comparing the profiles of the work presented in different performances with the score. The score may in the first instance help us to reject those profiles in which the sound base is not in accord with the given data. But once we have rejected these patently defective performances (these profiles of the work) we are normally still left with a number of performances in accord with the score but different among themselves with regard to details unspecified in the score but normally closely tied to the aesthetic value of the work concretized in performance. Which performance then are we to choose as being faithful and supplying us with that "original"? Thus, a confrontation of performances with the score does not provide an answer to this question.

As long as we maintain the position that a musical work (say, Chopin's B Minor Sonata) has as its aesthetic object a unique, wholly determined, univocal profile—the "ideal aesthetic object" the composer undoubtedly wishes to realize—so long does the quest for the "most faithful" performance, were it to exist, remain futile. At first glance it appears that the composer himself might successfully undertake such a quest since—as is supposed—he alone knows that ultimate artistic profile with which he intends to endow his work. But, strictly speaking, before the performance of his work, even the composer himself does not know the profile in all its qualifications; at best he imagines it more or less precisely and at times he may merely be guessing at it. With regard to symphonic works it is probably always the case that it is difficult to imagine the complex profile of an orchestral work in all its detail and full tonal coloring. After the performance of the work, even if the composer accepts the performance as realizing his artistic intentions, there is no guarantee that he has not made a mistake. And after the composer's death, particularly if he has not left any recordings, we can never be certain of the nature of that aesthetic object dreamed of by the composer.

With the score subjected to full analysis and a certain number of "correct" performances, we now realize that we have to change our approach to the whole question. A musical work, understood as an artistic product of its composer, is first a schema designated by the score, second a determined multiplicity of possibilities designated by the areas of indeterminacy of the schematic product—each providing in realization one of the work's profiles. And each such profile may be realized within a certain class of identical, or at least similar, correct performances. It may be that in composing his work, the composer has in mind only one among all these possible profiles; nevertheless, his creation extends beyond his artistic intentions, allowing other possible profiles of the work that, precisely on account of a certain imprecision in the score and, by not fully determining the work, open up the possibility of its realization in many ways. The actual performances of a work need not exhaust all the possibilities defined by the work in the sense of a schema designated by the score. They may not even realize the "best" possible profiles of the work. But as long as the sound base revealed in the performance is in accord with what the score designates and if, moreover, all the remaining qualities of the work revealed in performance do not extend beyond the possibilities of the work as a schema, then every performance fulfilling those conditions is "proper," even though not all these performances reveal equally valuable profiles of the work and even though they reveal profiles such as the composer himself had not envisaged. Naturally, the concrete profiles of the work regarded as legitimately belonging to the one schema constitute a multiplicity of *mutually exclusive* products; nevertheless, the whole group is bound together by the schema designated by the score.

Given such an understanding of a musical work, the problem of its identity disappears, since we are no longer concerned with a *single* object that in historical time undergoes certain changes arising from shifting historical conditions. But such an understanding is available only in philosophical analysis that reveals the true nature of a musical work. In daily commerce with a musical work we are normally unaware of its special structure. The process of communing with one and the same work imposes upon us a totally different conception: namely, that it is one and the same object, which endures in historical time but undergoes gradual change. Then once more we have the question of what is permissible. What boundaries of change must be recognized for preservation of the identity of the musical work thus understood?

It is clear that not every musical work as a schema designates an equally rich multiplicity of possible, concrete, aesthetically valuable profiles of the work. In this respect some works may be very rich, others less so, and still others quite impoverished. It does, however, appear certain, because of the incomplete nature of musical scores, that every work as a schema designates *some* multiplicity of possible concrete profiles. The multiplicity depends not only on the degree of the schematism of the work—that is, partly and indirectly on the degree of precision in the scoring—but also on the kind of multiplicity of possible completions of the work as a schema that is designated by the work's areas of indeterminacy. It would be premature to assert that the richer the work is in concrete profiles, capable of realization in various performances, the higher is its artistic value, for this value depends not only on the multiplicity of these possibilities but also on the level of aesthetic value of the work's profiles realized in specific performances. But it is surely true that a work rich in its possible aesthetically valuable profiles has a chance of a longer life—that is, of numerous performances and hearings in a number of epochs.[5] Each epoch may discover a profile of the work that best suits its taste and may embody that profile in performances usually assuming (wrongly!) that the profile it has chosen is the only "proper" profile and therefore is the work itself. Without discovering through philosophical analysis the characteristic schematic structure of the work that designates the above-mentioned multiplicity of possibilities, we tend to treat as an absolute the profile of the work that appears most valuable to us, identifying it with the work itself.

If, at an earlier stage, I had already been obliged to accord the musical work a purely intentional character, so now, when it has turned out that, as a reflection of the score, it is a schematic object, also possessed of a certain multiplicity of possibilities (including a certain multiplicity of possible concrete profiles), I see even more clearly now that the work is a purely intentional object. No real, individual object can be either such a variously indeterminate schema or a multiplicity of possibilities pertaining to that schema, which moreover are supposed to be embodied in performances realized in individual and real acts. But this is a very specialized ontological problem that I cannot here pursue.

The discovery of the various concrete profiles of a work, all of them belonging to a single schema, is a matter either of a detailed scientific analysis of the work on the basis of its score, or, so to speak, of musical experiment carried out by

---

5. A chance only, because in fact the life expectancy of a work is not wholly determined by the work itself but also by various independent circumstances that influence the formation of musical cultures and the artistic taste prevailing in their midst.

specific performers. It is also true that there are listeners who, in the course of attending to a particular performance, are capable of achieving an aesthetic experience such that the heard performance will reveal a profile of the work of which the performer is ignorant.

Taking into account the different mode of listening to and perceiving musical works and diverse aesthetic experiences not only complicates the whole theoretical position but reveals yet another aspect of the problem of the identity of a musical work in historical time. A single performance of a particular work, for example, in a concert hall full of people, may be presented to particular listeners in very different ways, depending upon a variety of circumstances in which the listeners' perceptions and accompanying aesthetic experiences develop. These circumstances include the particular listener's anatomic/physiological properties, his psychosomatic state during performance, his musical and musicological competence, his artistic sensibility and education, the auditorium and the surrounding audience, but above all also the listener's own emotional life and the manner in which he is capable of isolating himself from it during the concert. All this has a bearing on the process of perception and correlatively on the manner in which the final individual concretion of the work constitutes itself for the particular listener. The circumstances may be quite different for two listeners sitting side by side. But it is precisely this concretion of "the same" performance of a particular music work that is the immediate musical reality in which every listener participates and upon which he formulates convictions regarding the particular work. However, various details provided through the performance in the given concretion of the musical work are either faultily grasped (perhaps through an improperly read line of a certain melody) or remain unnoticed or ignored during perception. Or certain emotional qualities foreign to the work may be imposed upon it or another time the whole work shorn of any such qualities, and so on.

As a consequence, the profile of the work as a whole in performance undergoes a more or less profound alteration in relation to what it ought to be in any given performance. We are, however, rarely aware of these shifts. Spontaneously, we trust our own aesthetic experience, and, therefore, the work constitutes itself in the manner in which it appears to us. Thus, the variety of profiles in which a particular work reveals itself concretely to the listener grows considerably. We may also have the case wherein a work is perceived as a stereotype shared with other works, causing the variety of profiles to diminish considerably. Yet it is with reference to the work as it appears to us, in a concretion achieved in the course of a certain aesthetic experience, that we formulate our opinion of it in concepts and judgments. And instead of referring this opinion to the concretion that we immediately perceive, or at least to the performance of the work, we most frequently refer it uncritically and without adequate justification to the work itself. When the opinions formulated on the basis of the concretions of the work then vary from one listener to another, disputes arise over attempts to describe (and even more so attempts to evaluate) a work heard in one and the same performance. Sometimes people arrive at shared opinions regarding either the work's properties or its values. In the course of debates among experts and lay listeners there gradually emerges a collectively formulated and accepted opinion regarding a work's character, and correlatively there emerges a single, intersubjective, dominant aesthetic object, constituting the equivalent no longer of the opinions of one listener, but of the musical public in a given country at a given time. The work—we may call it a social object—becomes an element of the world surrounding that society, like other objects that surround us and are also intersubjective objects available to a whole society.

Just as in the case of real objects we assume that these objects change with certain characteristic changes in the data of experience, so also musical works appear to us to undergo a change when an intersubjective opinion with reference to them undergoes a significant change. Naturally enough, of course, real objects exist autonomously and possess specific qualities independently of the type of opinions formulated by people experiencing them. On the other hand, musical works, as specific intersubjective aesthetic objects, exist solely by intentional fiat (of creative acts, instructions within the score, or the listeners' conjectures), that is to say, heteronomously. With regard to their properties they are ultimately dependent upon the opinions we hold of them. These opinions acquire the character of guiding ideas that not only influence listeners in their listening habits (and therefore in their concretions of a given work) but also dictate to the performers how they are to play the work. This is apparent in the influence of musical academies on their pupils, in the pressure of critical opinion upon young performers, and in other ways. Outstanding performers liberate themselves to an extent from this influence when, contrary to prevailing opinion, they introduce a new interpretation of the work, and thus exposing the public to their performances, begin to affect individually the public's guiding idea of a given work.

Both the changes in the guiding idea held by the listeners and the changes in the prevailing type of performance of the same work create the impression that the work itself is changing over time. With the passage of time, both listeners and performers are no longer able to recall the original, or at least the earlier, profile of the work. It seems to them that the work has adapted itself to the new performances and to a fresh guiding idea. This gives rise to a specific historical process (at least apparently) of a slow transmutation of the musical work as a dependent, intersubjective aesthetic object. There follows the question as to what are the permissible limits of such transformation if the identity of the work is to be retained. This question is, as we have noted, unanswerable as long as we do not refer back to the score and the work as a schema, which it designates with the cluster of possibilities regarding its concretion in a variety of ways. By referring back to the score we discover not only a different conception of the work as such—a specific suprahistorical work even though the moment of its creation is historically determined and is itself part of history—but simultaneously it transpires that the very problem of identity (understood so that it takes shape only if one follows a historical process of change in a purely intentional, intersubjective object) is a pseudoproblem.

The historical process of the apparent changes in the musical work is in fact only a process of discovery and concretion of new possibilities for different profiles of the work leading to the acceptance of one of them as particularly valuable and "unique," and to an analogous treatment of a different profile of the work in the next epoch in which, in turn, this new profile enjoys exceptional prestige. As long as the score exists, this process may include a consciously conducted return in the performances and aesthetic experience to previously abandoned profiles of the work. There may also be a certain restraint with regard to deviations in performance, since the score clearly marks the boundaries whose transgression means that we no longer are dealing with a different (though permissible) profile of the same work, but simply with a different *work*. Where there is no score—as before the invention of musical notation—we are dealing with a historical process of the work's changes. Therefore, despite a tradition maintained within the consciousness of a certain musical culture, there may come about the performance and perception of a work that is different from the original and from the originally intended. But in those circumstances we lack the means to ascertain either that the identity of the work has been retained or that it has been broken.

It appears that this discussion applies only to the circumstances of musical works in previous epochs, before they could be fixed in authorial recordings. In principle, we can now play the authorial rendering countless times on the same record, always comparing it with performances by other interpreters and judging the extent to which these depart from the work created by the composer. But it seems to me that this alters the theoretical situation only to the extent that we now can assure ourselves that the composer was lucky enough, on a particular occasion, to succeed in performing his own work and imprinting upon it that particular profile. Even if we know this, we may reach the conclusion that the profile of the work realized by its composer is neither unique nor perfect and that in fact there are several permissible variations in the performance of his work. The composer's artistic achievement is not so much the realization of a unique model performance but rather the creation of the work as a schema subject to musical notation that, as I have already argued, displays a variety of potential profiles. Modern techniques of preserving performances do not so much allow us to return to the work itself as an "original," but to one of its possible profiles realized by the composer. The fact that this realization happened to be the effort of the composer rather than of a performer may be of great historical significance, but it is of little consequence for a philosophical theory concerned with musical works.

In the light of these remarks we may consider it no cause for regret that in the historical development of music the dominant system of preserving musical works was the score. For it was precisely the certain imperfection of this system—as it appeared to us initially—namely, the incomplete determination of the work by the score, that has this advantage over preserving the work by recording: that it reveals the essential structure of the work, that is to say, on the one hand the "fixed" relatively[6] invariant schema, and on the other hand, the multiplicity of the possible various profiles through which a work may manifest itself. This approach also enables us to understand how the specific structure of a musical work distinguishes it from works of painting and architecture.

This is the way I perceive, more or less, the most important problems connected with the musical work at the threshold of a philosophical exposition of its specific structure, its mode of existence, and such of its properties as have a fundamental significance for bringing about the concretions of aesthetic values during specific performances. I am well aware that this is only a beginning and that only cooperation between a philosophically inclined musical theorist and musicologists trying to achieve a deeper understanding of the objects of their particular research into actually existing musical works can push the matter forward and eliminate the many difficulties that are bound to emerge in the course of further investigation.

Paris 1928—Lwów 1933—Kraków 1957

6. It is "relative" because it contains an element of indeterminacy caused by the shifts in the qualities of musical sounds themselves in the light of possible changes in the technical structuring of instruments.

Roman Ingarden
and His Time

MAX RIESER*

When Roman Ingarden died suddenly on June 14, 1970, the body of his writings on philosophy of art was certainly more extensive than that of any other Polish thinker of his time. It also encompassed almost half of his output of writings on philosophy. The other half consisted of his famous treatise *Controversy about the Existence of the World,* which was directed against the epistemology of idealism; one volume deals with the history of contemporary philosophy, basically with that of Edmund Husserl, but also with that of Henri Bergson (his doctoral dissertation), Franz Brentano, Max Scheler, and in a very critical negative sense with neopositivism, the bête noire of his philosophizing. Yet despite the copiousness of his aesthetical studies, he stated[1] three months—to the day—before his death, at a lecture in Amsterdam on March 13, 1970, that his two main works on philosophy of art did not even mention aesthetics but were called *Investigations on the Borderline of Ontology, Logic and Literary Criticism* and *Investigations on the Ontology of Art.* The reason, he said, for this striking omission was that these two books were first supposed to serve as a preparation for dealing with certain general philosophical problems, notably the issue of realism versus idealism. "The specifically aesthetic questions," Ingarden continued, "were to me at that time of secondary importance . . . it was clear to me from the start that we should proceed in aesthetics not in an empirical-inductive way but work out an eidetic view of a general idea of a work of art and of the less general ideas of the works of the particular arts." In other words, Ingarden asserts that he wanted to perform this task as an epistemological phenomenologist. A

Reprinted from *The Journal of Aesthetics and Art Criticism* 39, no. 4 (Summer 1971), by permission.

*A resident of New York City and a frequent contributor to journals of philosophy and aesthetics, the late Max Rieser was a lifelong friend of Roman Ingarden.

1. *Bulletin International d'Esthétique* 5, no. 14 (Nov. 1970): 5.

few explanatory remarks are here in order. The first title mentioned by him, *Das literarische Kunstwerk,* was really the subtitle of his work written in German. The second title he gave in 1960 to a book of essays translated from Polish and forming basically the contents of the second volume of his *Studies from Aesthetics,* published in 1957–58 and dealing with the following subjects: Musikwerk, Bild, Architektur, Film. These studies on the particular arts were originally to be included in *Das literarische Kunstwerk,* but they became too voluminous for this purpose and were expanded in the course of almost thirty years. There was in addition a further work, *On the Cognition of the Literary Work,* written before World War II and published in German in 1968. Shortly after the end of World War II, Ingarden published "Sketches from the Philosophy of Literature" (Łódź, 1947), which are partly contained in *Studies from Aesthetics,* the first volume of which was *On the Cognition of the Literary Work. Studies* includes also a very short essay, "On the Ontology of the Literary Work of Art" (pp. 249–55), which is an adjunct to the study *On the Cognition of the Literary Work.*

But we still do not know why a work on philosophy of art like *Das literarische Kunstwerk* should in any way affect the issue of realism versus idealism. This seems rather strange. Ingarden wrote the book with an oblique look at the idealistic epistemology of Edmund Husserl. He wrote the book in 1927–28 and showed the manuscript to Husserl when he passed through Freiburg im Breisgau in January 1928 on his way from Paris to Poland. In fact, Edith Stein, who was the assistant of Husserl (and later was dragged by the Nazis from a Dutch Catholic convent and killed in Auschwitz), helped Ingarden to smooth out the German version stylistically. (The Polish version was done only after World War II by Maria Turowicz and published in 1960.) Ingarden wanted to show here that the literary work of art was an "intentional object" and even the model of such an object, while Husserl considered also the material objects as "merely intentional," i.e., as "nothing," and therefore was gravely mistaken. Ingarden wanted also to demonstrate that the work of art was a "schematized" creation which, in order to become an object of aesthetic enjoyment, required a "concretization" by a listener (or observer) whose contribution was essential in this respect. The work of art needed, in addition, a *material object* in which it was funded. Thus material objects and the minds of the creator as well as the receptive experiences of the enjoyer of art were needed for the constitution of aesthetic objects. All in all an independent material world—apart from other minds—was the indispensable prerequisite of the literary work of art. This is the meaning Ingarden had in mind when he declared that the issue of realism against idealism was his primary concern when writing his aesthetic study. Although Ingarden was one of the most devoted pupils of Husserl, he never adopted his so-called transcendental idealism and he tried until 1927 to convince him of his error. Ingarden, in 1918 after his return to Poland from his university studies in Freiburg, wrote a long letter to Husserl stating that he was deeply troubled because of this difference of opinion. He was also convinced—against the opinion of other pupils of Husserl—that Husserl at the beginning of his philosophical career as a pupil of Franz Brentano in Vienna was also a realist, but later on might have changed his mind under the impact of the idealistic tradition of German philosophy. Ingarden himself was a pupil of Husserl in Göttingen and Freiburg from 1912 till 1917 (with interruptions) and it was in this period that his philosophical convictions were solidified. Husserl's ideal was philosophy as a "rigorous science" but he could make it so only by adopting the "phenomenological reduction," by looking at the world as phenomenon of one's own consciousness, and by turning away from the material things as "merely intentional" creations: they had no autonomous being but were merely correlates of our units of meaning; they were constituted on the basis of the so-called aspects of things succeeding themselves in an unending stream. Although this variety of idealism admitted the existence of other minds and the intersubjective acts of behavior, it went much farther than Berkeley or Fichte.

Ingarden accepted the eidetic method of Husserl, i.e., the method of attempting to find the "essentials" of a thing, but he rejected the transcendental idealism of Husserl in *Das literarische Kunstwerk* and in a long series of letters and essays. This was also the concern of his main epistemological work, *Controversy about the Existence of the World,* which he started writing in German in 1937 in order to show the manuscript to Husserl. But Husserl died the following year and Ingarden continued it in Polish during World War II. It was published soon afterwards (in 1947–48) through the Polish Academy of Sciences in Cracow, of which he was already a member before its transfer to Warsaw. Thus it could be said that Ingarden practiced epistemology in his two main works: in a circumstantial way in his first work (*Das literarische Kunstwerk*) and in a direct way in his second work (*Controversy about the Existence of the World*). But it should be stressed that while he stood for epistemological realism, he still opposed all forms of neopositivism, empiricism, and materialism. He translated *Controversy* into German, so that many of his writings are available in that language. This is understandable because his two main works are in a sense a "pendant" to the phenomenological writings of Husserl, for whom there was little interest in Polish philosophy. Many years after World War II, Ingarden stated that when Maria Turowicz undertook its translation into Polish, there was not a single copy of *Das literarische Kunstwerk* in the libraries of Warsaw. He complained also of the brutal ignorance and open hostility with which his writings were received there. He was better known in Germany and even in France. He was the first in Poland to practice a new form of aesthetics: the epistemology of art based on and derived from phenomenological ontology with concepts couched in the idiom of phenomenology. These conditions changed in Poland to some extent. Neopositivism, which he rejected so energetically, lost its dominant position and instead Marxism came to the fore. Pre-war psychologism, which he opposed, had also a bourgeois tinge, so that the posture of phenomenology underwent a change, although the Marxists continued to condemn it. But since neopositivism was much more influential, the hostility of the Marxists first attacked it. Ingarden was impervious to exterior events. He condemned any intervention of the state into philosophical matters but stayed silent. After the war the interest in his aesthetic philosophy in Poland grew much stronger. He was one of a handful of survivors of the great era of Polish philosophy in the twenties and thirties. From 1926 until 1941 he was professor of philosophy in his home city of Lvov, where the rebirth of Polish philosophy started in 1895 with the appointment to the chair of philosophy of Kazimierz Twardowski, a pupil of Franz Brentano and a native of Vienna, educated at the prestigious Theresianum and docent at the University of Vienna.

Ingarden's *Das literarische Kunstwerk* was published in Halle an Saale at the height of the economic crisis in Germany in 1931. At the end of the next year the National Socialists came to power in Germany. Ingarden's revered teacher Edmund Husserl was ousted from his position, and instead of being a famous professor of philosophy and a *Geheimrat* of the Weimar republic, he became a tracked man who had to publish his writings abroad—for instance, in Belgrade—and hold a public lecture in Vienna. He was originally, like Kazimierz Twardowski and Ingarden himself, an Austrian subject; all three were educated in Austrian schools and deeply affected by the cultural ambiance of the old Austrian Empire. Husserl was no ethnic German but a native of Moravia (like Sigmund Freud). Ingarden won a professorship at Lvov University in newly created Poland in 1926 but had to cease his lectures in 1941 with the Nazi occupation of Poland, when all universities were closed and over twenty professors of the university and of the Technical University of Lvov were shot without rhyme or reason.

Both Husserl and Twardowski died in 1938. After 1945 conditions were very different. Lvov was ceded to Russia, and Ingarden was appointed to the chair of philosophy in Cracow University, which was never dominated by neopositivists as the University of Warsaw had been. As for Husserl, his library and the enormous legacy of writings were saved from Nazi destruction by being transported to Louvain in Belgium, where the Husserl archives were established. Husserl was now a world-famous historical figure whose posthumous works were published in Holland. He had an enormous influence on the philosophy of continental Europe and in fact fathered not only the phenomenological existentialism of Martin Heidegger but also that of Jean-Paul Sartre and Merleau Ponty.

The essentials of the philosophy of art of Ingarden have a number of fundamental points: (1) the work of art as an "intentional" object; (2) the stratification of the work of art; (3) its concretization by the listener or reader.

(1) The intentionality of the work of art means that it has no independent existence like material objects, nor is it an ideal object like a triangle; it must have a material subsoil in tone, marble, ink spots, etc.

(2) The multiple stratification of the work of art, especially of the literary one, is its most basic characteristic, which, if neglected, leads to errors, as we know from the history of criticism. The idea of mental strata of different depth is a characteristic of phenomenological philosophy. Human life itself has a number of such strata and they may be the model of the strata of the literary work of art. The "constitution" of what we call an object may also be composed of strata. Thus, for instance, the macrophysical idea of the material object and the microphysical one of the same object are two strata of the same thing. We may also speak of different layers of things if a person relates on the theatrical stage a story which does not refer to the events happening on the stage but to events happening elsewhere. According to Ingarden's basic theory the stratification of the literary work of art is fourfold.

It was, of course, never doubted that a poem had two sides: the words that had meanings and especially in poetry the sound of those words played an important role in the constitution of the poetic work. We could interpret that as two strata of the poem. But Ingarden's system goes much farther. It states that the four strata in question are: the sounds of the words; the meaning of the sentences into which the words are combined; the schematized aspects of the presented objects; and the represented objects themselves. Every stratum makes its contribution to the aesthetic status of the whole work. The whole forms a sort of polyphony of aesthetic quali-

\ties. The type of this polyphony determines the aesthetic value of the work. The structure of these strata and their connection determine the organic character of the work. The latter may be created by the mental processes of the author but it is neither a part of his psychology nor of that of the reader or listener. Even if it has no independent existence like material things, it still has the semiautonomous existence of intentional things. Ingarden is very careful in warning against psychologizing the work of art as Husserl was careful against psychologizing logic after he had been sharply rebuked by Frege for having committed such a sin in his *Philosophy of Arithmetic* (he was a mathematician by training). Although theoretically speaking the literary work of art consists of four identifiable strata, Ingarden asserts that the second stratum—that of the meaning of the sentences—is the central one since without it there would be no work at all. The units of meaning constructed by the verbal network largely determine the two other strata, that of schematized aspects of the objects represented and that of the objects represented themselves. They decide the question whether the work be historical, naturalistic, symbolical, etc. The type of sentences also decides another question: whether the work is clear or unclear. If the work lacks clarity, the obscurity might also be intended and mysteriousness may be a value in an aesthetic sense. (I would observe here that mysteriousness, obscurity, equivocality have emerged as an aesthetic value since Romanticism; in antiquity and, for instance, in French classicism obscurity was rejected as a poetical value and clarity as exalted in this field.)

The essential fact about the sentences of the literary work, according to Ingarden, is that they are not true propositions in a logical sense—as, for instance, those of a scientific treatise or of a newspaper report—but merely quasi-propositions; optative statements are merely quasi-optative, imperatives are quasi-imperative, questions are merely quasi-questions, etc., because this is not a real world but a world of fiction. As the persons of the literary world are fictitious, their statements are merely quasi-statements. This concept of quasi-statements caused a lot of controversy because the critics maintained that literary works reveal a sublime type of truth and this assumption seemed menaced by Ingarden's theory. This was, however, an error since Ingarden was concerned merely with the technical, logical status of the literary sentences, not of their ulterior meaning. This question has little aesthetic importance since all literary works, i.e., mainly novels, are composed of such sentences regardless of their aesthetic value. In the discussion of the first stratum, i.e., of the word sounds, Ingarden discusses many questions of linguistics but these questions as well as the logical disquisitions have now a historical value since they are concerned with theories that were current at the time of the writing, i.e., in the twenties. On the other hand, the purely aesthetic issues may still be topical and fresh.

How about the two remaining strata of schematized aspects of represented objects and of the represented objects themselves, which are certainly unusual in literary criticism? It should be first stated that this is not any disclosure of facts but a philosophical interpretation due to an analysis of the functions of the literary work. It can be better understood if it is considered in terms of the phenomenological philosophy. According to the latter's epistemology the objects of the so-called material world appear to us in a succession of variously differing aspects, depending on our position in relation to them. These aspects may repeat themselves indefinitely; the material thing really needs an infinity of descriptions but we never achieve a definitive knowledge of it; it cannot be described in absolute terms. In an intentional work of art the author also constructs his represented objects in a series of aspects but he may and even must select them in a definitive way to describe the thing he has in mind. In the real world the multiplicity of aspects culminates in a certain unit of meaning that we graft on the so-called material thing; in the literary intentional object the sequence of aspects constitutes the thing of artistic imagination. But this composite picture is schematized because the author must leave out many details; he will not, for instance, always tell whether his hero has blond or dark hair, etc. The picture is therefore always incomplete; it awaits, so to speak, the work of "concretization," i.e., recreation and completion, to be performed by the listener or reader. This indeterminacy of the work of art is combined with the further quality of the sentences of the literary work that they may also be equivocal or, so to speak, opalescent. All this results from the fact that the objects represented have no material existence but are a part of a world of fiction. Just as in the real world, the objects are built up by means of their looks as they are appearing, so in the work of art, the world of represented objects, which form the last or fourth stratum, are built up by the aspects emerging out of the sentences. The two last strata of the literary work of art really reflect the state of affairs that, according to phenomenological philosophy, happens in the material world.

According to the Marxist aesthetic view, the relation of art to reality is the main problem of aesthetics since the work of art should be a concentrated generalized view of that reality. This problem would be here the object of the fourth stratum of Ingarden's concept of the literary artistic object, although Ingarden never mentions Marxist philosophy before World War II. The stratum of represented objects should represent the actual world, life, or reality. Ingarden deals at length in this connection with the concepts of space and time as imagined in the work of art and as different from what is called space-time in the world of physics or in the experience of living beings. He then reaffirms what was said about the indeterminacy of the aspects in saying that the world of represented objects must contain undetermined spots because the work cannot afford an infinity of descriptions. What is in the work cannot be fully described or fully individualized; it is a schematized picture with inherent lacunae.

The form and the succession of the aspects determine the style of the work—whether it is expressionistic or impressionistic, whether the succeeding scenes follow in a succession of abrupt explosions, or whether they are shading off imperceptibly in a continuous melodic stream of words. The stratum of represented objects is important for another reason: it reveals—and this is one of the main functions—what Ingarden calls the metaphysical qualities of the work, namely, whether the work in question is tragical, comical, charming, seducing, etc. These are the qualities of the human existence. Our everyday life is in general grey and without outstanding features and we desire something that would lend it color and significance. Of course, we may become aware of these qualities of our existence in real life but then, if that happens in the humdrum of daily life, it may cause us suffering and great distress. But the works of art may show them to us and therein we may contemplate them in serenity and detachment. In other words we may discover in them the hidden sense of our existence. It is very significant that Aristotle devoted his main essay on poetics just to these metaphysical qualities.

One of the most important terms of Ingarden's philosophy of art is *concretization*. We have heard that the work of art is a schematized picture that has empty spots requiring completion. It is this completion that the listener or reader accomplishes in the process of concretization. He plays therefore an active role in the whole aesthetic process. His contribution is indispensable if the work of art is to become an object of aesthetic enjoyment, if from an artistic schematic frame it is to become an aesthetic object. Ingarden stresses the active part of the listener or reader in the constitution of the aesthetic object. The whole question of subjectivity and objectivity in the evaluation of the work of art gets thereby a new dimension. Ingarden devotes much space to this analysis in his second work on aesthetics, *The Cognition of the Literary Work*. His translations are in general full of emendations and additions. According to this discussion the concretization of the work of literary art by the reader is based on its reconstruction after the reading. If the reconstruction is not faithful or not complete, the concretization will be equally faulty. He must also grasp the hierarchical structure of the work since not all its parts are of equal weight. The concretization consists basically as was said in the filling in of the spots of indeterminacy of the work and in the aesthetic experience of it. The result of this process may be then disclosed in aesthetic judgments. Now if the concretization or any of its phases are faulty, the aesthetic judgment is also erroneous. The work of art is an intersubjective object but the concretizations are monosubjective or individual and they can scarcely be of equal importance or correctness. This fact explains the diversity or sometimes even the contradictoriness of aesthetic judgments since what the reader or the critic judges is not the work as such but his concretization or concretizations. Therefore, for instance, the literary critic also judges his concretization when he writes his criticism, and the more encompassing his concretization would be, the more prospects there are of a correct aesthetic judgment on his part. Ingarden is therefore an opponent of "easy skepticism" in philosophy and especially of "relativism" in aesthetics, and I remember well how he rose to his feet at the XI Congress of Philosophy in Venice to refute such relativistic statements of Étienne Gilson.

What Ingarden calls the stratum of represented objects is generally considered the content of the work of art, but it is apparent in his theory of stratification that he rejects the division into form and content as equivocal and the concept of form as vague. It is obviously undeniable that the representation of the things and objects is effected by means of their aspects or looks. In that respect Ingarden is in the footsteps of the phenomenological conception of material things: they are also formed by successive aspects. We may mention here that Ingarden rejects, in a study on "Poetics" written around 1940, the view of the Russian formalists, notably of B. Tomashevskii, that poetics is merely a part of linguistics since the poetic language is merely an artistic variety of common speech. This is an error according to Ingarden because this view omits the two important strata of schematic looks and of represented objects in the literary work and narrows down its import; there are even opposite views that language plays no part at all in the literary work, its substance is merely its meanings. This of course Ingarden does not accept since he thinks that the word sounds play an important role in the literary work as against the scientific work, for instance, which also is composed of words, but here the sounds of words are immaterial; they may be even detrimental to the transmission of knowledge if we devote too much attention to them in such a work. If we look closer into Ingarden's conception of the fourfold stratification of the literary work of art, we may become aware that this structure represents to some extent the fourfold structure of the human life in its totality. The first two strata of sounds and of the schematized meanings of the sentences represent our mental world of linguistic meanings, while the two other strata of the objects and their aspects represent the perceptively observable part of the human world, the things we see, hear, etc.

Any philosophy and especially a philosophy of art is marked by the characteristics of its time of origin and even very often by the works of art from which it derives its inspiration or abstracts its concepts. Ingarden considered his theory of literary art valid for all branches of that art, but he quotes in his basic work *Das literarische Kunstwerk* excerpts from Heinrich von Kleist and Novalis to show a diversity of styles; it seems to me, however, that the real model of his analysis was the works of Thomas Mann, namely, the novels *Buddenbrooks* and *Der Zauberberg*. As he was a man of vast erudition, many literary works were therefore present to his mind. To exemplify the foreshortenings of the time perspective of novels he quotes excerpts from Joseph Conrad's novel *Lord Jim* (see his *Cognition of the Literary Work*). As for the concept of "concretization" the most obvious example could be a theatrical piece concretized on the stage where its spots of indeterminacy are filled in—as Ingarden mentions himself—by the producer. He arranges the various rehearsals until his judgment is satisfied that the staging is adequate to the intentions of the author. Various kinds of staging may be equally acceptable but some may be closer to the spirit of the work than others of like quality. Even the form of declamation may be vital to this concretization. Thus the actors of the Comédie Française are sporting a certain traditional declamatory pattern when they declaim the verses of Racine inimitable to foreigners. But it should be made clear that Ingarden does not consider a drama as a purely literary work but one on the borderline of literature.

Ingarden's analyses of the other arts follow a similar conceptual pattern. Ingarden looks after their ontological basis. He also considered the fact of their stratification as central to their being intentional objects. He was therefore shocked—as he avers himself—when he became aware that the musical work had no manifold stratification but only one stratum— that of sounds. This seemed to contradict his theory of art. It would be interesting to inquire what is the reason for this "recalcitrant" behavior of music because it would perhaps illumine the whole concept of stratification. Ingarden himself never tried it. But the true reason is obviously the fact that the so-called strata are by no means a part of the material substratum of the arts but something beyond and above it, something existing only in the world of meanings. Thus, for instance, the colored surfaces of a painting (*das Gemälde*) are by no means a part of the strata of the painting, its strata are—just as in the literary work—the schematized aspects and the represented objects. Thus the strata of the painting are really beyond it.

Ingarden himself was a musician; he played the piano and fulfilled thereby the ideal of an aesthetician according to a remark Irwin Edman once made during a speech to the effect that an aesthetician should be familiar at least with two arts. As a musician Ingarden could not find the familiar world of meanings in "absolute music" and he rejected the contention that music "expresses" or "represents" (*vorstellen*) something. This was done also by many other things and would be too little as the whole achievement of the wonderful works of music.★ The musical work is not temporal in the sense of its performances but quasi-temporal, as is also the work of literature, in that it develops in phases that often determine each other in a reciprocal way; it is not an ideal object like mathematical numbers because it has a genesis in time, but once terminated by the composer, all its parts exist simultaneously and its phases are quasi-temporal. They are in no connection with the real cosmic time, they possess their own musical time, they are completely impervious to the reality surrounding them even if they have a historical origin and bear its mark. A musical work contains nonsonorous qualities, for instance, aesthetic ones; it may contain emotional qualities like terror, awe, etc. It may also express the author just as a performance may express the performer, but this goes beyond and above music; program music may even represent something; for instance, the fire motif in *Rheingold* of Richard Wagner portrays fire but then it must be materially similar in some way to fire; but these are not necessary properties of music. A performance of a musical work cannot be identified with the work itself; it is merely its concretization and the score fixes the musical text only incompletely; the performance is called upon to fill it in. The "forms" within the work are figurational (*gestaltist*) within the terms of figurational psychology (*Gestaltpsychologie*). Conditions, and even the instruments on which it is played, change, but the musical work preserves its identity, and certain properties of its parts constitute the wholeness of

---

★ED. NOTE: Rieser here seems to be saying that expression and representation are accomplished by many other things besides music. Thus, they fail to explain the wonderfully unique gifts of this art.

such works as a sonata or a symphony; certain anticipations and transitions in sound do it or even its contrast or its emotive similarity, etc.

Ingarden stresses the difference between the material substratum of a painting—its canvas, the spots of oil and ink, and their chemo-physical properties—from the painting as a picture, i.e., an artistic object. As such it has "strata" although fewer than the literary work of art: 1) the stratum of aspects (reconstructed or constructed looks); 2) the represented objects or situations; and 3) if the painting has a literary or a historical content, there is a third stratum, because without it we cannot fully understand the painting, its prehistory, its consequences, etc. The represented objects appear through their aspects but they are not a sequence as in literature but a selection effected once for all. The aspective stratum is not complete, it is partly undetermined as the whole painting is an intentional object. The observer must fill in the lacunae of the aspects in his concretization. Some aspects are constructional—they are indispensable for the construction of the objects; some are decorative—they embellish through colors or other particulars the objects represented; but sometimes the same aspects fulfill both of these functions. While in literature the central stratum is that of the meaning units of the sentences, here the aspects are the main stratum since without them there is no painting. The spiritualistic character of the theory of stratification is apparent. The represented objects and the literary content of the painting are in the world of meanings and do not belong to the picture strictly speaking. As for the aspects, they are part of the artistic object but not of its material substratum (the painted spots on a canvas). Ingarden states that the cubist painting lacks the stratum of the aspects because the cubists tried to paint the essential structure of the represented objects and neglect its aspects. An ordinary landscape without "a story" would have two full strata but not three. Ingarden regrets in a footnote that Heinrich Woelfflin was not aware of the stratification of the work of art (painting). But the spiritualistic ontology of the phenomenological theory would not have enlightened him about the empirical style of the paintings since it would apply anyway to all paintings regardless of style or value. Abstract paintings have only one stratum; since the strata of so-called aspects and of represented objects are lacking here, it could be said that the method of stratification does not apply; the only remaining problem is whether the painted surface (*Gemälde*) really becomes a painting in the artistic sense (*Bild*). All paintings may embody what Ingarden calls the metaphysical qualities (the tragic, the graceful, the charming, etc.).

Ingarden applies the methodology of stratification and concretization also to the remaining arts: he does not discuss sculpture but he does architecture extensively. Architecture is the best example of an art whose material substratum coincides with its artistic form but cannot be identified with it. The building is a heap of stones; it becomes a church through the act of consecration and a work of art if we regard it in an aesthetic attitude. Everybody must not look at it in this attitude and then he will not see in it a work of art.* Ingarden calls it in his technical, phenomenological idiom an intentional object but he could say also that the work of art is a spiritual object since its artistic quality is in the world of meanings attributed to it. But remaining within the limits of his terminology, we state that it is an intentional object since it has no independent existence but must have a material basis—its stones. Following in the footsteps of those theoreticians who declared that architecture is "frozen music," he states that the work of architecture more closely resembles the musical work than the other visual arts, despite its totally different structure, because as art it has no representational component; its whole artistic content could be intuited in its lines just as music is in its sounds. It has, however, unlike music, two strata: 1) a potentially unlimited number of "aspects"; and 2) its tridimensional form. The aspects constitute in a painting its most important stratum while here it is the tridimensional shape which is the most important.

The building may of course have also some painterly *valeurs* but they should accentuate, not cover up or overwhelm its architectural shape. The shape in question is organized on geometrical, not on organic, principles, as would be equations with a limited number of variables, and it is the unity of this organization that makes for its artistic value. It is the concretization of geometrical shapes. It is as such nontemporal although it has an origin in time; some call it even exclusively spatial. Architecture and absolute music are not reproductive but most creative of all the arts and express most intimately human faculties and human nature. Like a painting without a literary story, the silent film has also two strata. Abstract paintings, like music, have only one stratum.

Despite his rejection of psychologism in aesthetics in 1958 Ingarden wrote an essay "On the Role of Language in a Theatrical Play," which states that the words in a drama should be considered as actions since they form a part of the action of the drama; they prompt it by communication, by expression, and by influencing the partners of the play. But Ingarden

*ED. NOTE: Rieser is apparently saying that not everyone will look at a building this way, and therefore will not be looking at it as a work of art.

was first and foremost an epistemologist and an ontologist; his aesthetics were part of his epistemology. In his *Literary Work of Art*, he dealt with its fictive and spiritual being and in his *Controversy about the Existence of the World*, with the being of the latter. His philosophical position in Poland was difficult as Poland was dominated in the twenties and thirties by neopositivism and after World War II by Marxism. He became docent at the University of Lvov in 1925 at the age of 32 and professor in 1933. Eight years later all the universities in Poland ceased to function. In 1945 Ingarden was appointed to the chair of philosophy at the University of Cracow but was demoted from this position in 1951 by a decree of the Communist government of Poland. When I saw him at the Istituto Cini in Venice in 1956 he had behind him a six-year interdiction from teaching, lecturing, and publishing that struck all prewar bourgeois professors who did not teach logic that was ideologically neutral. We see therefore a gap in Ingarden's publications from 1948 to 1958 when the State Office of Scientific Publications began to publish his *Philosophical Works*. But Ingarden stayed silent, he never complained. There are only two footnotes in his writings on the subject of Marxist philosophy. If the latter contends, he said, that philosophy is the basis of all the sciences, then a prioric philosophy (like his own) is more apt to provide such a basis than the positivism of the nineteenth century which considered philosophy merely as a sort of synopsis of the sciences. "A prioric" in Ingarden's terms does not mean the Kantian a priori, but simply a truth evident to reason. For instance, if we say that the color orange is between yellow and red, this is an a priori statement. Elsewhere he defends himself in a footnote against the reproach of "idealism" (the standard accusation of Marxist-Leninists). He says that he cannot be an idealist if he assumes the existence of intentional objects because this implies the existence of real objects also. This means of course that he is no idealist in an epistemological sense but does not exclude opposition to materialist philosophy. Ingarden used the enforced leisure to make a translation of Kant's *Critique of Pure Reason* into Polish. Such translations were paid according to length and published. When he was seventy years old, he had to retire from his teaching position and in the following years he translated his writings into German; these were published in Tübingen. His last publication was the correspondence with Husserl and his remembrances of Husserl published by the Husserl archives in The Hague. A grant from the Ford Foundation made it possible for him to visit America with his wife. He was not very happy here. He had a number of lectures at American universities but his mastery of English was limited and the philosophical climate of the country was totally uncongenial to him—it was the realm of that neopositivism that he criticized in Poland in the thirties but incomparably more powerful. He told me later on that his sojourn in this country was a total loss. But Marvin Farber, editor of the "American Lecture Series," included in this collection "Times and Modes of Being," an excerpt from Ingarden's *Controversy about the Existence of the World* (Springfield, Ill.: Charles C. Thomas, 1964). Before that his essay "The Hypothetical Proposition" was published in Marvin Farber's *Philosophy and Phenomenological Research* (18, 4 [1958]). I also placed in 1960, in the special issue of *The Journal of Philosophy* devoted to Polish philosophy, an excerpt from Ingarden's writings. Ingarden lectured at the Summer Meetings in Alpbach (Tyrol) where students from some socialist countries for the first time heard about phenomenology. He lectured about this subject at the University of Oslo, Norway, and received the Herder Prize for his philosophical activities promoting friendship among nations. He received this prize at the University of Vienna where he also gave two lectures at the International Congress of Philosophy in September 1968, one on aesthetics, the other on general philosophical subjects, but he declined to take part in August 1968 at the last International Congress of Aesthetics in Uppsala, stating in a letter to me that the selection of the program ("Art and Society") was a "scandal," meaning an undue limitation of subject matter. While he was considered in Germany almost a native writer, he was very important to Polish philosophy and culture in general as the founder of the epistemology of art. He was Poland's greatest philosopher of art and also a metaphysician of European rank. He had in this respect an unusual gift of precision, a constructive ability rarely encountered in addition to his indefatigable industry. He was no idealist in the epistemological sense but a spiritualist in aesthetics; he considered art a spiritual value. He had an almost poetical sensitivity to the arts as when he described the beauty of the "aspects" of Notre Dame in Paris in the delicate haze of the morning sun, in midday splendor, and in the violet shadows of the dusk. When he broadcast a radio address at the hundredth birthday of Edmund Husserl, he stated with sadness how much influence philosophy had lost since Husserl's lifetime. He was one of the last illustrious pre-World War I figures, raised and formed in one of the greatest epochs of European civilization.

Select Bibliography

Works by Roman Ingarden in English Translation

"Aesthetic Experience and Aesthetic Object." Translated by Janina Makota and Shia Moser. *Philosophy and Phenomenological Research* 21, no. 3 (1960): 289–313.

"The General Question of the Essence of Form and Content." Translated by Max Rieser. *Journal of Philosophy* 57, no. 7 (1960): 222–33.

"Reflections on the Subject-Matter of the History of Philosophy." Translated by Elaine P. Halperin. *Diogenes: An International Review of Philosophy and Hermeneutic Studies,* no. 29 (1960), pp. 111–21.

"A Marginal Commentary on Aristotle's *Poetics.*" Translated by Helen R. Machejda. *Journal of Aesthetics and Art Criticism* 20, nos. 2 and 3 (1960–61): 163–73, 273–85.

"Artistic and Aesthetic Values." Translated by H. Osborne. *British Journal of Aesthetics* 4, no. 3 (1964): 198–213. Reprinted in *Aesthetics,* edited by H. Osborne (Oxford, 1972), pp. 39–54.

Time and Modes of Being. Translated by Helen R. Machejda. Springfield, 1964. [A selection of extracts from a major work by Ingarden (so far untranslated in full) whose title, normally rendered *Controversy over the Existence of the World,* I give as *Does the World Exist?*—A. Cz.]

"The Physicalistic Theory of Language and the World of Literature." Translated by Maria Pelikan. *Yearbook of Comparative Criticism* 2 (1969): 80–98.

The Cognition of the Literary Work of Art. Translated, with an introduction, by Ruth Ann Crowley and Kenneth R. Olson. Evanston, 1973.

The Literary Work of Art: An Investigation on the Borderlines of Ontology, Logic, and Theory of Literature. Translated, with an introduction, by George G. Grabowicz. Evanston. 1973.

"On So-Called Truth in Literature." Translated by Adam Czerniawski. In *Aesthetics in Twentieth-Century Poland,* edited by Jean G. Harrell and Alina Wierzbiańska (Lewisburg, 1973), pp. 164–204.

"Phenomenological Aesthetics: An Attempt at Defining Its Range."

Translated by Adam Czerniawski. *Journal of Aesthetics and Art Criticism*
33, no. 3 (1975): 257–69.
Man and Value. Translated by A. Szylewicz. Washington, D.C., 1984.

Commentaries

Eagleton, Terry. *Literary Theory: An Introduction*. Oxford, 1983.
Falk, Eugene H. *The Poetics of Roman Ingarden*. Chapel Hill, 1981.
Magoliola, Robert R. *Phenomenology and Literature: An Introduction*. West
Lafayette, 1977.
Ray, William. *Literary Meaning: From Phenomenology to Reconstruction*.
Oxford, 1984.
Wellek, René. *Four Critics: Croce, Valéry, Lukács and Ingarden*. Seattle and
London, 1981.
Wellek, René, and Warren Austin. *Theory of Literature*. New York, 1949.

Index

Compositor:	Harrington-Young Typography & Design
Text:	11/13 Bembo
Display:	Bembo
Printer:	Edwards Brothers
Binder:	Edwards Brothers